The Behaviour Change Wheel

A Guide to Designing Interventions

Susan Michie
Lou Atkins
Robert West

Endorsements

It is often said that behaviour change is easy. It isn't. But help is at hand. This excellent book provides a step by step guide on how to do it. The authors recognise the practical things which that need to be done. This wisdom is derived from the authors' deep understanding of the scientific evidence. This book is a major resource and should be read by all commissioners and practitioners whose work involves behaviour change.

Professor Mike Kelly, *Director of the Centre of Public Health, National Institute for Health and Care Excellence (NICE)*

Policy makers, practitioners and researchers need a guide to designing behaviour change interventions which is simple but does not oversimplify. Michie, Atkins and West provide an excellent step-by-step guide based on their extensive experience and expertise, using their COM-B model. They take the user through the science and the practical, real-world considerations with valuable examples and worksheets for each step. This is likely to become the basic interdisciplinary guide to designing behaviour change interventions, for a diversity of behaviours in a wide variety of contexts, in the UK and internationally.

Professor Marie Johnston, *Emeritus Professor of Health Psychology, University of Aberdeen*

All scientists, students and practitioners designing behaviour change interventions recognise the highly complex set of decisions that must be made to be effective. Yet many of us engage in our professional trades of behaviour change interventions—whether these trades be in research, in practice, in policy, or in teaching—by simply following the unsystematic but helpful advice of our own mentors or teachers about how to design these interventions. This book offers insightful, rigorous, and standardised ways to approach behaviour change intervention development, that once read, is astonishing in its clarity and usefulness.

Professor Karina Davidson, *Professor of Behavioural Medicine in Medicine, Cardiology, and Psychiatry, Columbia University*

The Behaviour Change Wheel is a powerful new tool for those designing and evaluating behaviour change interventions. By setting out a systematic method for understanding behaviour, and linking this understanding to techniques known to change behaviour in a clear and engaging format, this book gives practitioners and policy-makers a scientific approach to designing interventions that are most likely to be effective. Professor Michie and her colleagues have done the field a great service by providing a step-by-step guide to designing behaviour change interventions, which will prove particularly useful in the area of public health.

Professor Kevin Fenton, *Director of Health and Wellbeing, Public Health England*

This is a highly practical workbook for helping practitioners develop and organise behaviour change interventions. But it is much more than that. It is a framework for thinking about behaviour change designed to not only change individual behaviour, but also to optimise the behaviour of change agents. It is simply the best attempt I have seen to lay out a taxonomy of behaviour change, from characterising the behaviours to change, through the specific techniques to produce the change, to the contextualising factors. I suspect that in future it will be seen as doing for behaviour change what Linnaeus started many centuries ago for biology.

There are some things that when you see them you wonder "Why hasn't someone done this before?" This is one of those ideas.

This book operationalises the intuitions of good intervention developers and implementers in ways that should make all of us better at the trade.
Professor Ron Borland, Nigel Gray Distinguished Fellow in Cancer Prevention at Cancer Council Victoria

It's great to see some of the most important recent advances in behaviour change intervention design all in one book. The COM-B model and theoretical domains framework are excellent tools for analysing behaviour. Professor Michie and her colleagues are leading the way in demonstrating a truly scientific approach to the selection and application of behavioural constructs to intervention design.
Anna Sallis, Behavioural Insights Research Advisor, Public Health England

Contents

Acknowledgements

Grateful thanks go to Marie Johnston for her pioneering work in behaviour change, her helpful comments on earlier drafts and for writing the Foreword for this book.

We are grateful to the researchers whose work forms the basis of the case studies in this book.

We would also like to thank our colleagues in the Health Psychology Research Group and the Tobacco and Alcohol Research Group at University College London for their helpful comments on earlier drafts and to Anna Sallis at Public Health England. Thanks also to the participants of many seminars and workshops whose feedback has helped shaped this book.

Website

See **www.behaviourchangewheel.com** for updates.

Foreword

By **Professor Marie Johnston, Emeritus Professor of Health Psychology, University of Aberdeen**

Changing people's behaviour is an important aim for policy-makers, healthcare providers, educators, researchers etc., but the task is challenging and all the necessary resources are rarely available. Even when we know what we are trying to achieve, we may lack the time, the multidisciplinary team, access to the people whose behaviour needs to change, understanding of behaviour change theories or knowledge and skills relevant to changing behaviour. It is therefore timely for the publication of this book which will enable non-specialists to design an intervention to change behaviour.

The book presents a high level of scientific evidence and theory in a very practical, accessible, usable format. It takes the reader through eight steps, each with full explanations, worked examples and the worksheets necessary for the reader to do the developmental work for a new intervention. The initial steps enable the reader to clearly specify the behaviour that is the target of the intervention, followed by an introduction to a simple method of analyzing what needs to change first using the COM-B model: is greater Capability, more Opportunity or stronger Motivation required? Having identified what needs to change, the reader is guided through a series of judgements about how best to achieve change, e.g. by education, persuasion, training or changing the environment, before considering how policy such as fiscal policy or service provision might facilitate the process. The next stage builds on the science of behaviour change and offers a wide range of techniques that are the active ingredients of every behaviour change intervention. Finally, decisions are made about how to deliver the intervention – e.g. when and how often? is it best face-to-face, by internet or in some other way?

The whole process offers a valuable combination of scientific theory and evidence with practical judgements about the affordability, acceptability etc of the planned intervention. So it is well-suited to the real-world settings in which behaviour and behaviour change interventions occur.

The authors draw on decades of experience of designing and implementing behaviour change programmes for diverse clients in a wide range of settings. They are highly esteemed in the academic sphere as leading behavioural scientists, as practitioners who have delivered effective behaviour change interventions and as policy advisors to various bodies including several UK government departments. The resulting book is just what is needed in this field - a basic interdisciplinary guide to designing behaviour change interventions for a diversity of behaviours in a wide variety of contexts.

Introduction

'There's nothing as practical as a good theory'
Kurt Lewin

Changing ingrained behaviour patterns can be challenging. The same is true for one-off behaviours where one is working against a strong psychological, social or environmental gradient. This book is a practical guide for designing and evaluating behaviour change interventions in these cases. It uses the Behaviour Change Wheel (BCW), a synthesis of 19 frameworks of behaviour change found in the research literature [1].

The BCW has at its core a model of behaviour known as COM-B. The initials stand for 'capability', 'opportunity', 'motivation' and 'behaviour', and the model recognises that behaviour is part of an interacting system involving all these components. Changing behaviour will involve changing one or more of them in such a way as to put the system into a new configuration and minimise the risk of it reverting. The BCW identifies different intervention options that can be applied to changing each of the components and policies that can be adopted to deliver those intervention options.

For example, if one wished to reduce the propensity of young drivers to engage in risky driving practices (e.g. driving too fast), one should canvass all the options including improving their 'capability' to read the road and adjust their driving to the conditions, restricting their 'opportunity' to drive recklessly by means of speed limiters or speed humps, and/or establishing whether a promising approach would be to try to change their 'motivation' to drive safely through mass media campaigns or legislation and enforcement. Any or all of these may have some effect but the BCW provides a systematic way of determining which options are most likely to achieve the change required.

Intervention options in the BCW are described in very general terms. A much more specific description is provided by a taxonomy of 93 'behaviour change techniques' (Behaviour Change Technique Taxonomy (v1); BCTTv1) that has recently been developed [2] and specific taxonomies of behaviour change techniques (BCTs) in domains such as behavioural support for smoking cessation [3-9]. This Guide provides a brief introduction to the generic 93-item taxonomy, BCTTv1, and its application.

Some readers of this Guide may be familiar with another behaviour change framework that is related to the BCW: the Theoretical Domains Framework (TDF) [10]. This has become popular, particularly when it comes to changing clinical practice. The TDF can be thought of as a variant of the COM-B model which subdivides the components in a particular way. This Guide will show how the components of the COM-B model and domains of the TDF are linked.

In medicine there exists already a guide for intervention design and evaluation that covers behaviour change: The MRC Guidance on Complex Interventions [11]. This guidance describes a process of iterative intervention development from theory and evidence synthesis, through initial pilot testing to field tests, implementation and evaluation. The BCW is designed primarily to assist with the first part of this process. However, it can be used all the way through when it comes to understanding why a particular intervention strategy is or is not meeting expectations.

The key benefit of using the BCW is that it encourages intervention designers to consider the full range of options and choose those that are most promising through a systematic evaluation of theory and evidence. It is not a panacea, or even a blueprint, for behaviour change, but a system for making the best use of the understanding and resources available to arrive at a strategy.

A companion to this book, 'ABC of Behaviour Change Theories' [12] summarises 83 theories of behaviour and behaviour change identified in a cross-disciplinary review involving psychology, anthropology, economics and sociology (www.behaviourchangetheories.com).

Who the Guide is for

This Guide is for policy makers, intervention designers, researchers and practitioners: in fact, everyone with an interest in systematically applying theory and evidence to designing and evaluating behaviour change interventions. It is designed to be useful for people from a wide range of disciplines with varying levels of expertise. However, intervention designers are encouraged to work with psychologists or other behavioural scientists where possible in developing, delivering and/or evaluating behaviour change interventions.

If one thinks of intervention design as like playing a game of chess, this Guide is an introduction to the opening moves. It should get designers off to a good start. It is not a substitute for a detailed understanding of the behaviour in question but a way of harnessing whatever understanding exists and identifying valuable areas for extending that understanding.

Although most of the examples in this Guide are from the area of health, the method is applicable to behaviours across all domains, for example, environmental sustainability, pro-social behaviour and policy implementation.

Why have we written this Guide?

Over several decades we have been involved in the development and evaluation of behaviour change interventions in areas as diverse as road safety, addiction and infection control. It has become apparent that much, if not most, intervention design uses the 'ISLAGIATT' principle (a term coined by Martin Eccles, Emeritus Professor of Clinical Effectiveness). The letters stand for 'It Seemed Like A Good Idea At The Time'. This principle encapsulates an approach in which the intervention strategy is arrived at before having conducted a thorough assessment of the appropriate behavioural target(s), what it would take to achieve change in these and how best to implement this. Instead, personal experience, a favoured theory or cursory analysis is used as the starting point for intervention design often leading the intervention designer down a fruitless path.

14

There have been several attempts to be more systematic about intervention design, involving frameworks that draw attention to a variety of options and in some cases to ways of selecting these from an analysis of the behaviour change problem of concern. These include MINDSPACE [13], an approach favoured by the UK government, and Intervention Mapping [14] an approach that has been adopted in a number of other countries. Unfortunately none of these frameworks cover the full range of intervention options available that may be important and indeed are covered by other frameworks. Therefore, we reviewed all the frameworks we identified in a systematic search and developed one that brought together all the relevant components, and linked them in a way that should allow for a comprehensive and systematic approach to intervention design.

In less than three years since the paper introducing this method was published it has been accessed more than 43,000 times, cited in other publications more than 140 times and there have been numerous requests for seminars and training in how to apply the BCW in a wide variety of contexts. We therefore decided that it would be helpful to develop a manual that could expand on the original paper, filling in gaps in the process, and providing additional tools for analysing behaviour and choosing intervention functions and policy categories.[1]

The BCW was developed, not only to aid intervention design, but also to improve the process of intervention

[1] Seminars and workshops intended to accompany this Guide are offered by the UCL Centre for Behaviour Change (www.ucl.ac.uk/behaviour-change). For more information contact behaviourchange@ucl.ac.uk or follow on Twitter @UCLBehaveChange

evaluation and theory development. It provides a systematic way of characterising interventions that enables their outcomes to be linked to mechanisms of action, and it can help to diagnose why an intervention may have failed to achieve its desired goal. For example, the English Department of Health last year paid some £80 million to GPs to incentivise them to provide smoking cessation advice to their patients. Yet, time series analysis has shown no detectable effect on behaviours that would be expected to arise from such advice such as provision of prescriptions for stop-smoking medicines [15]. A simplistic analysis may lead to the conclusion that the incentives were enough only to encourage GPs to 'game' the system so that they could receive the payments without actually doing the necessary work. A COM-B analysis and the BCW provides a way of addressing the issue more broadly by also addressing issues of capability (e.g. how to raise the topic of smoking in a way that is comfortable and rewarding) and opportunity (e.g. how to fit the advice into a very narrow time window).

More about the Behaviour Change Wheel (BCW)

The BCW was developed from 19 frameworks of behaviour change identified in a systematic literature review [1]. As noted earlier, none of these frameworks were found to be comprehensive. In addition, few of them were conceptually coherent or clearly linked to a model of behaviour change. Some of the frameworks assumed that behaviour was primarily driven by beliefs and perceptions, while others placed greater emphasis on unconscious biases and yet others focused on the social environment. Clearly, all of these are important and needed to be brought together in a coherent manner. The BCW aimed to address these limitations by synthesizing the common features of the frameworks and linking them to a model of behaviour that was sufficiently broad that it could be applied to any behaviour in any setting (see Appendix 1 for more information on frameworks contributing to the BCW).

The BCW consists of three layers. The hub of the wheel identifies the sources of the behaviour that could prove fruitful targets for intervention. It uses the COM-B model for this. Surrounding this is a layer of nine intervention functions to choose from depending on the particular COM-B analysis one arrives at. Then the outer layer, the rim of the wheel, identifies seven types of policy that one can use to deliver these intervention functions (Figure 1).

Figure 1 The Behaviour Change Wheel

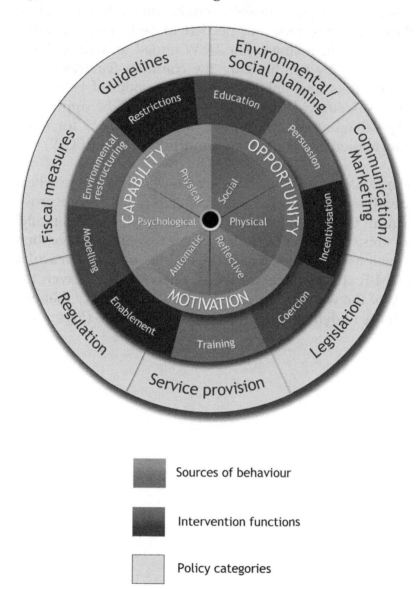

Readers may wonder why we use the term intervention 'function' rather than intervention 'type' or 'category'. The reason is that the same intervention may have more than one function so interventions cannot be classified in this way, only characterised. For example, a mass media campaign to promote smoking cessation may contain an element that is educational (providing new information on the harms of smoking) but also be presented in a way that is intended to be persuasive (generating feelings of worry about the health harms of smoking). Thus it would be unhelpful to classify the mass media campaign as either educational or persuasive; it would be more accurate to say that it performed both educational and persuasive functions.

The importance of distinguishing between intervention functions and policy options is not always immediately apparent so an example may help. Suppose one is seeking to reduce the rate at which GPs prescribe antibiotics for sore throats. Then suppose that a COM-B analysis suggests that increasing GPs' capability to resist what they perceive as pressure from patients to issue a prescription is an important target. This in turn suggests that they would benefit from better understanding of how reducing antibiotic prescribing might be achieved, through the intervention function, education. However there are several different ways in which this might be achieved. One might be through issuing guidelines; another might be a marketing approach, for example through articles in professional magazines or through websites. Yet another approach might involve providing a service in which trained facilitators visit and explain and demonstrate what is required and how to achieve it. The BCW can help prevent foreclosing on the decision before analysing what would be the best approach or combination of approaches.

It is important to understand that the COM-B model and BCW applies at any level from individuals to groups, sub-populations and populations. When applying it to groups and populations the components are construed in terms of aggregate parameters, e.g. proportion of the target population drinking above recommended limits, understanding the harmfulness of excessive consumption, wanting to reduce population consumption etc. When applying the model to organisations with an internal structure in terms of communication and influence, these are captured in terms of physical and social opportunity. However, for some behaviour change problems these can be further elaborated to capture specific features of these parameters (e.g. patterns of diffusion of influence).

An exercise that evaluated the BCW as a method for describing the wide range of explanatory factors identified in three literature reviews of non-adherence to medication reached the following conclusions: "COM-B provides a more comprehensive explanation of adherence than existing models. First, it includes automatic processes such as habit ... Secondly, it explicitly includes factors at a systems level ... Thirdly, the specificity of components within the COM-B model, and hypothesised relationships between them, allows a precise description of the relationship between individual determinants and adherence, making it easier to identify appropriate interventions." [[16] p12].

The authors also make the important point that COM-B is helpful for ensuring that the intervention designer does not get drawn into thinking on only one level (for example individual or systems level). They also found that not all factors identified in the literature review fitted into exactly one COM-B component but might have their effects via a number of components, giving the examples of depression, substance abuse, marital status and forgetting. This points to the need to investigate how a particular factor has its effect in order to generate clear hypotheses about processes which, in turn, inform the intervention.

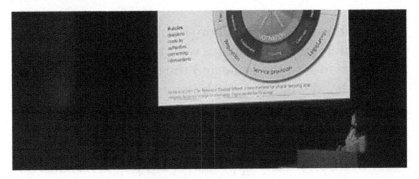

Things to remember

There are several important things to remember when using this Guide:

- Just like any science, the science underlying behaviour change can only take you so far with complex real-world problems. Most intervention strategies will require judgement on the basis of the best available evidence. Criteria for using judgement at various steps in the intervention design process are set out in this Guide and case studies illustrate how judgement has

21

been applied to make decisions on intervention content and delivery. Moreover, the conditions underlying the behaviour can change. This means that there is no substitute for direct evaluation of interventions by the most rigorous method practicable.

• Drawing on judgement and first principles can provide a method for designing interventions in the absence of relevant evidence of an effective solution to a behaviour change problem. However, it should not replace the use of evidence where it is available.

• The time and resources one should put into developing an intervention strategy will be influenced by the importance of the issue and the needs of the situation. Clearly, developing a strategy to increase physical activity rates in the population will merit a more in-depth and resource intensive analysis than getting one's teenage son to go for a cycle ride. However, in both cases, a BCW approach could pay dividends.

Intervention design is about more than effectiveness

All behaviour change interventions operate within a social context. Thus effectiveness is only one consideration when designing an intervention. Table 1 introduces the APEASE criteria for designing and evaluating interventions or intervention ideas. This Guide focuses on effectiveness because if interventions are not effective the other considerations do not apply. However, it will clearly be important to consider the other factors.

Table 1 The APEASE criteria for designing and evaluating interventions

Criterion	Description
Affordability	Interventions often have an implicit or explicit budget. It does not matter how effective, or even cost-effective it may be if it cannot be afforded. An intervention is affordable if within an acceptable budget it can be delivered to, or accessed by, all those for whom it would be relevant or of benefit.
Practicability	An intervention is practicable to the extent that it can be delivered as designed through the means intended to the target population. For example, an intervention may be effective when delivered by highly selected and trained staff and extensive resources but in routine clinical practice this may not be achievable.
Effectiveness and cost-effectiveness	Effectiveness refers to the effect size of the intervention in relation to the desired objectives in a real world context. It is distinct from efficacy which refers to the effect size of the intervention when delivered under optimal conditions in comparative evaluations. Cost-effectiveness refers to the ratio of effect (in a way that has to be defined, and taking account of differences in timescale between intervention delivery and intervention effect) to cost. If two interventions are equally effective then clearly the most cost-effective should be chosen. If one is more effective but less cost-effective than another, other issues such as affordability, come to the forefront of the decision making process.

Table continued.

Acceptability	Acceptability refers to the extent to which an intervention is judged to be appropriate by relevant stakeholders (public, professional and political). Acceptability may differ for different stakeholders. For example, the general public may favour an intervention that restricts marketing of alcohol or tobacco but politicians considering legislation on this may take a different view. Interventions that appear to limit agency on the part of the target group are often only considered acceptable for more serious problems [17].
Side-effects/ safety	An intervention may be effective and practicable, but have unwanted side-effects or unintended consequences. These need to be considered when deciding whether or not to proceed.
Equity	An important consideration is the extent to which an intervention may reduce or increase the disparities in standard of living, wellbeing or health between different sectors of society.

How to use the Guide

Chapters 1 to 3 of the Guide describe a step-by-step method for designing behaviour change interventions. These are summarised in Figure 2. Although the process is described in linear terms, it is clear that it may involve cycling back and forth between steps as one discovers issues and obstacles. Thus it is important to be flexible in the application of this approach.

Figure 2 Behaviour change intervention design process

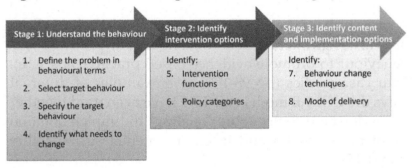

Case studies and worksheets are provided at the end of each step to help translate principles into practice (blank worksheets are provided in Appendix 2).

The case studies are intended to show the range of applications of the COM-B model, TDF, BCW and taxonomies of BCTs in both intervention design, evaluation, forming conceptual models and informing policy.

Case studies of the COM-B model (pp 76-86) show how it has been used to understand behaviours in context (Box 1.11) and develop conceptual models of behaviour in context (Box 1.12); as a first step in designing interventions (Box 1.13); to inform government policy (Box 1.14).

Case studies of the BCW (pp 131-134, pp 144-145) show how it has been used to: promote uptake of evidence-based guidelines through the selection of intervention functions based on a COM-B analysis (Box 2.2) and describe policy and guideline content (Box 2.4).

A case study of the TDF (pp 96-97) shows how it has been used to design interventions to change health professionals' behaviour to promote evidence-based practice (Box 1.16). Four case studies (pp 98-105) give examples of different ways the COM-B model and TDF have been used together to understand behaviours relating to implementation problems in health and in environmental sustainability (Box 1.17).

Case studies of taxonomies of BCTs (pp 164-173) show how they have been used to inform policy (Box 3.2) and specify intervention content based on: formal theories (Box 3.3); TDF (Box 3.4); and both COM-B and TDF (Box 3.5).

Look out for these boxes containing key principles and learning points to help you throughout the book

BCW is a method not a magic bullet!

When attempting to change behaviour we want the answer to the question 'what is going to achieve my goals?' Sometimes we will have access to 'off the shelf' interventions that have been found to work for similar problems. But more often we will need to design the intervention for our particular circumstances. We can do this by starting with a behavioural analysis of the problem, making a behavioural diagnosis of what needs to change and then linking that diagnosis to intervention functions and BCTs to bring about change. In that sense, this Guide is not a 'magic bullet' saying what works in which context but a method for finding that out.

Questions addressed by the Guide

There are eight steps in the design process which cover: understanding the behaviour (Chapter 1); identifying intervention options (Chapter 2); and identifying implementation options (Chapter 3). They address key questions:

Chapter 1
- Step 1: What is the problem you are trying to solve?
- Steps 2-3: What behaviour(s) are you trying to change and in what way?
- Step 4: What will it take to bring about the desired behaviour change?

Chapter 2
- Steps 5-6: What types of intervention are likely to bring about the desired change?

Chapter 3
- Steps 7-8: What should be the specific intervention content and how should this be implemented?

The importance of devoting sufficient time and resources to the first three steps in order to select, specify and fully understand the behaviour to be changed cannot be overstated. If the assessment is not thorough, the formulation of the problem is less likely to be accurate, and the intervention less likely to be effective.

To take a medical analogy, if a doctor does not conduct a thorough assessment of a patient's symptoms, an accurate diagnosis is unlikely to be made and therefore the treatment may be wrong. For those who are not convinced of the need to spend resources on the preliminary assessment, one could ask if they would appreciate being given a cursory assessment for chest and abdominal pain and prescribed an indigestion remedy, when they are experiencing symptoms that may signal a heart attack.

Chapter 4 provides a real world example of applying the methods described in Chapters 1-3 to intervention development. Chapter 5 presents tools for understanding and changing behaviours that can be used to evaluate interventions and synthesise evidence.

The Appendices contain additional information about the BCW and BCTTv1, blank worksheets for the output from each step in Chapters 1-3 and answers to a BCW quiz.

Chapter 1: Understand the behaviour

This chapter covers the four steps that lay the groundwork to understanding the 'target behaviour'. Step 1 - define the problem to be addressed in behavioural terms; Step 2 - select the target behaviour(s), i.e. the behaviour(s) most likely to bring about change to address the problem; Step 3 – specify the target behaviour in as much detail as possible; Step 4 – identify what needs to shift in order to achieve the target behaviour.

Step 1. Define the problem in behavioural terms

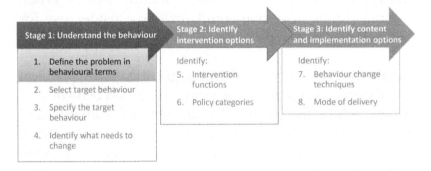

Stage 1: Understand the behaviour	Stage 2: Identify intervention options	Stage 3: Identify content and implementation options
1. Define the problem in behavioural terms	Identify:	Identify:
2. Select target behaviour	5. Intervention functions	7. Behaviour change techniques
3. Specify the target behaviour	6. Policy categories	8. Mode of delivery
4. Identify what needs to change		

Why define the problem in behavioural terms?

Defining the problem in behavioural terms means being specific about i) the target individual, group or population involved in the behaviour and ii) the behaviour itself.

For example, we might want to address environmental or health problems such as there being too much traffic, high rates of obesity, or infection rates in hospitals. However, stating the problems in this way does not indicate what behaviours we are trying to change or whose behaviour is involved.

Too much traffic involves car use but car use is also a consequence of car purchasing. Addressing the problem may require changing one or other or both of these. When it comes to car use, one could further consider use for particular journey types.

Weight loss is not a behavioural target; increasing physical activity and reducing calorie intake are broad behavioural targets while increasing the amount of walking and reducing consumption of high fat foods are more specific targets. One may be more specific and specify 'walking to and from work' or 'walking at least two miles each day'. The nature and specificity of the behavioural target will be important in determining how far the problem of overweight is solved.

Infection rates are not a behaviour. A number of different behaviours may be relevant, including hand-washing, effective use of protective clothing, cleaning surfaces, maintaining appropriate isolation etc. As with the other examples, each of these can be specified more precisely.

Worked examples

A worked example is given, together with a worksheet, at the end of each step. You are encouraged to select a behaviour change problem relevant to your work and use the worksheets to design an intervention to address this problem.

How to define the problem in behavioural terms - completing Worksheet 1

Worksheet 1 contains three tasks: 1) identify as specifically as possible the behaviour or behaviours that need to be changed to solve the problem; 2) specify the location(s) in which the behaviour occurs 3) specify the individual, group or population involved. We will take one of the examples above: hospital staff hygiene practices. Box 1.1 shows an example of a completed worksheet.

Box 1.1 Example of a completed Worksheet 1

What behaviour?	Improving hand hygiene practices in all opportunities identified by national or local guidelines
Where does the behaviour occur?	Hospital wards
Who is involved in performing the behaviour?	Hospital nursing staff

Now it's your turn!
Please complete Worksheet 1

Step 2. Select the target behaviour

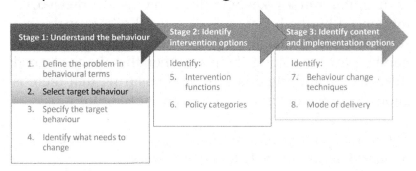

Stage 1: Understand the behaviour	Stage 2: Identify intervention options	Stage 3: Identify content and implementation options
1. Define the problem in behavioural terms	Identify:	Identify:
2. Select target behaviour	5. Intervention functions	7. Behaviour change techniques
3. Specify the target behaviour	6. Policy categories	8. Mode of delivery
4. Identify what needs to change		

Why select a target behaviour?

Behaviours do not exist in a vacuum but occur within the context of other behaviours of the same or other individuals. These interact as a system.

> Behaviours are part of a system – they do not occur in isolation

What might seem a simple set of behaviours, such as hospital nurses keeping their hands disinfected, is influenced by the behaviours of several others, including senior doctors disinfecting or not disinfecting, their hands, patients asking them whether they have cleaned their hands, and the domestic staff ensuring that there is enough alcohol gel in the dispensers (see Figure 1.2).

Figure 1.2 Example of nurse hand hygiene behaviours occurring within a system of behaviours

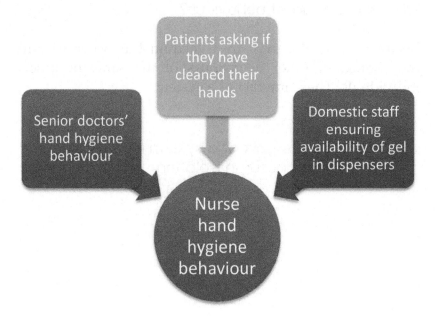

When considering which behaviour(s) on which to intervene, designers should think about all relevant behaviours performed by the target group or groups. If one selects a behaviour that is dependent on other behaviours, this needs to be taken into account in the design process as the intervention will need to target this set of behaviours. The inter-dependence of behaviours is shown in relation to eating healthily in Figure 1.3.

Figure 1.3 Behaviour as part of a system: the example of healthy eating behaviours

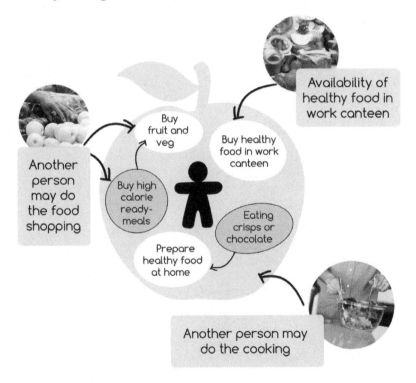

How to select a target behaviour

Start by generating a 'long list' of all the potential behaviours that may be relevant to the problem one wants to solve. An example is the behaviours that are relevant to reducing energy use in homes (Box 1.2). This can be reduced to a 'short list' using a systematic method (see next section). Having identified the core behaviours, the next step is to link them in a 'conceptual map', along the lines of the examples given in Figures 1.2 and 1.3.

Box 1.2 Listing candidate target behaviours

An example from the Townsville Residential Energy Demand Program (TRED Program)

Aim: To design an intervention to reduce residential energy consumption.

Method: A group of environmental experts listed potential target behaviours that could bring about lower energy use in the home.

Results: A total of 231 domestic energy reducing behaviours were identified:

* Reducing Electricity Consumption
  - Hot Water Systems - 24
  - Kitchen Appliances - 53
  - Entertainment Equipment - 18
  - Laundry Appliances and Bathroom - 28
  - Pools, Hot Tubs and Saunas - 7
  - Heating & Cooling – 40
  - Lighting - 17

* Complementing Energy Efficiency Behaviourswith Onsite Generation - 7
* Options for House Construction and Retrofit - 24
* Additional Behaviours related to Housing Construction – 13

Less is more!

It is worth considering that it may be more effective to intervene intensively on one or two target behaviours than to intervene less intensively on multiple behaviours.

Designers can select more than one target behaviour though it is advised to limit the intervention to just one or a few behaviours in the first instance. Introducing change incrementally and building on small successes can be more effective than trying to do too much too quickly; this is as true of organisational change as it is of individual change. It is important to remember that since each behaviour may have a different analysis (network of interlinking behaviours and COM-B analysis of each behaviour), an intervention should be informed by an assessment of all the relevant behaviours.

Having established which behaviours to target, the next step is to decide which to start with. There may be obvious indications as to which to choose, for example, from local knowledge or the research literature. The following criteria may be helpful in selecting the target behaviour:

1. The likely impact if the behaviour were to be changed.
2. How easy it is likely to be to change the behaviour; this will be influenced by local circumstances, for example, financial and human resources, acceptability and preference.
3. The centrality of the behaviour in the system of behaviours: thus, the positive 'spillover' effect if that behaviour were to be changed. Some behaviours are more 'central' in the system, and changing them is likely to have an impact on other behaviours, either positive in that it may support desired behaviour change or negative in that there may be negative consequences. Estimating this can be helped by gathering local evidence or by consulting the research literature.

4. Ease of measurement: if one wishes to evaluate the extent to which the intervention has changed the target behaviour, it should be measurable, either by routine data or by introducing new data collection procedures.

Applying these criteria to the example of energy reduction in the home, the behaviour of changing use of incandescent light bulbs to compact florescent bulbs may be judged to have:

1. moderate impact on energy demand reduction
2. high difficulty of change because of initial cost and aesthetics
3. moderate 'spillover' in that research has shown that changing one energy reducing behaviour is likely to encourage other energy reducing behaviours
4. high measurability, for example using numbers of compact fluorescent bulbs sold in local shops and self-reported use.

How to select a target behaviour - completing Worksheet 2

Worksheet 2 guides you through the process of rating likely impact, likely ease of changing the behaviour, spillover effects and measurability and using these ratings to guide selection of a target behaviour.

Worksheet 2 contains two tasks: 1) generate a 'long list' of candidates for target behaviours; 2) select the target behaviour based on a decision making rule for each criterion. Boxes 1.3-1.5 show completed examples of these tasks.

Box 1.3 Example of a completed Task 1, Worksheet 2

Task 1: Generate a 'long list' of candidate target behaviours that could bring about the desired outcome (in this example behaviours that could improve hygiene practices in hospitals)

Intervention Aim: improve hygiene practices in hospitals

Intervention designer response

Equipment
- Keeping sterile single use items in packaging until use
- Sterilising reusable medical equipment
- Handling sharps appropriately

Patient care
- Washing patients as appropriate, e.g. following incontinence

Hospital environment
- Cleaning wards, toilets, offices and theatres
- Changing bed linen as appropriate
- Transporting soiled or infected bed linen in bags
- Providing clean bed linen
- Emptying and cleaning commodes and bed pans following use
- Cleaning furniture including hospital bed frames and mattresses

Personal hygiene
- Cleaning hands using alcohol gel
- Cleaning hands using soap
- Providing alcohol gel
- Providing alcohol gel dispensers
- Providing soap
- Providing paper towels
- Wearing clean uniform
- Wearing personal protective equipment
- Providing personal protective equipment
- Covering mouth and nose with a tissue when sneezing

Box continued.

Waste disposal
- Disposing of clinical waste in appropriate containers
- Ensuring availability of clinical waste containers
- Emptying waste bins before they overflow

Task 2: Prioritise the behaviours by considering the following criteria:

1. How much of an impact changing the behaviour will have on desired outcome
2. How likely it is that the behaviour can be changed (when considering likelihood of change being achieved, think about the capability, opportunity and motivation to change of those performing the behaviour)
3. How likely it is that the behaviour (or group of behaviours) will have a positive or negative impact on other, related behaviours
4. How easy it will be to measure the behaviour

Different criteria will be more or less important in different situations. As a result of this prioritisation exercise, you are likely to reach one of the following decisions:

1. The behaviour appears very promising as a target behaviour
2. The behaviour is quite promising as a target behaviour
3. The behaviour appears unpromising but is worth considering as a target behaviour
4. The behaviour is not acceptable as the target behaviour (it doesn't matter what it is like on the other criteria, this behaviour cannot be selected as the intervention target)

Box 1.4 An example of prioritising behaviours

Keeping sterile single use items in packaging until use

The behaviour 'keeping sterile single use items in packaging until use' is estimated to be unpromising but worth considering in terms of impact because it is judged that if this behaviour were changed, it would not have much impact on improving hygiene practices in hospitals as it is mostly already adopted by relevant health professionals. It is considered to be very promising in terms of likelihood of change as it is thought that the behaviour would be easy to change as it is already widely adopted and so modelled by other health professionals and is part of hygiene protocols. It is estimated to be unpromising but worth considering in terms of spillover as it is judged that if this behaviour were adopted, it would not have any impact on other behaviours. It is estimated to be unpromising but worth considering in terms of ease of measurement as it would be difficult to monitor all instances of when packages were opened.

Cleaning hands using alcohol gel

The behaviour 'cleaning hands using alcohol gel' is rated as very promising in terms of impact because evidence suggests it is not always done by health professionals and would have a great impact on improving hygiene practices in hospitals. It is estimated to be promising in terms of likelihood of change as it is judged that it would be fairly easy to bring about change given that it is a behaviour performed mostly in public and would be influenced by social desirability effects. It is estimated to be promising in terms of a spillover as more health professionals washing their hands are likely to prompt colleagues and visitors to do so. It is rated as promising in terms of 'ease of measurement' as it would be fairly simple to monitor a behaviour that is routinely observed by others.

So the behaviour of cleaning hands using alcohol gel is selected as the target behaviour because after considering all criteria it appears to show the greatest promise.

Box 1.5 Example of completed Task 2, Worksheet 2

Potential target behaviours relevant to improving hygiene practices in hospitals	Impact of behaviour change[a]	Likelihood of changing behaviour[a]	Spillover score[a]	Measurement score[a]
Keeping sterile single use items in packaging until use	Unpromising but worth considering	Very promising	Unpromising but worth considering	Unpromising but worth considering
Cleaning hands using alcohol gel	Very promising	Promising	Promising	Promising

Record target behaviour here: Cleaning hands using alcohol gel

[a] Rate as: unacceptable, unpromising but worth considering, promising, very promising

Now it's your turn!
Please complete Worksheet 2

Step 3. Specify the target behaviour

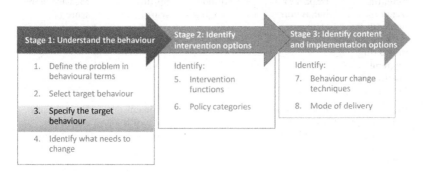

Why specify the target behaviour?

Having selected the target behaviour, the next step is to specify the behaviour in appropriate detail and in its context. The more precise you can be about the behaviour, the better the behavioural analysis is likely to be but clearly the greater the challenge in terms of assessing it. So, for example, 'eating less' will be less likely to help you decide what to do than 'cutting out snacks between meals and substituting fruit for puddings'; 'exercising more' will be less helpful than, say, 'engaging in brisk walking for one hour on Wednesday and Saturday each week'.

Specify the behaviour in terms of:
- *Who* needs to perform the behaviour?
- *What* does the person need to do differently to achieve the desired change?
- *When* will they do it?
- *Where* will they do it?
- *How often* will they do it?
- *With whom* will they do it?

48

Examples of behavioural recommendations that are too vague and more precisely specified alternatives are given in Table 1.1. These are taken from recommendations made by the NICE (the National Institute for Health and Care Excellence) with behaviourally specific alternatives generated by behavioural psychologists [18]. Following this BMJ article, NICE changed their methods so that recommendations are now made in behaviourally specific terms as described above.

Table 1.1 NICE recommendations in published guidelines on schizophrenia and more precise behavioural specifications [18]

Published main recommendations	Behavioural specifications			
	What	Who	Where[b]	When[b]
Acute day hospitals should be considered as a clinical and cost effective option for the provision of acute care, both as an alternative to acute admission to inpatient care and to facilitate early discharge from inpatient care	Encourage [offer?] acute day hospital treatment to inpatients or those facing acute admission to inpatient care	Service manager responsible for making treatment decision	In acute day hospitals in the UK	When patients are in or facing hospital admission
Cognitive behavioural therapy (CBT) should be available as a treatment option for people with schizophrenia	Offer cognitive behavioural therapy to everyone with schizophrenia	Trust board and health professional responsible for offering treatment options	In secondary and tertiary care	During formation of a care plan
Family interventions should be available to the families of people with schizophrenia who are living with or who are in close contact with the service user	Offer family intervention to all those in close contact with someone with schizophrenia	Trust board and health professional responsible for offering interventions to people in close contact with someone with schizophrenia	In community setting	Anytime

When providing family interventions, service users and their carers may prefer single family interventions rather than multifamily group interventions	Give information about and offer a choice of single family or multifamily group interventions when offering family interventions to people with schizophrenia or their carers	Health professional responsible for providing information to service users and carers about family interventions	In community setting	Anytime
For optimum effectiveness in preventing relapse, depot preparations should be prescribed within the standard recommended dosage and interval range	Prescribe depot preparations within the standard recommended dose and interval range [for all those with schizophrenia?]	Psychiatrist responsible for drug treatment	In community mental health team setting	During consultation with the patient

[b] These columns are in addition to the original paper by Michie and Johnston

Box 1.6 gives an example of specifying the target behaviour of administering oxygen to hospital patients at risk of developing septicaemia. This is the first step in the Sepsis Six care pathway [19]. This example also illustrates the number of behaviours that are associated with what seems initially to be a simple task.

Box 1.6 Specifying target behaviour

An example from behaviour in a care pathway to prevent inpatient mortality from sepsis [19]

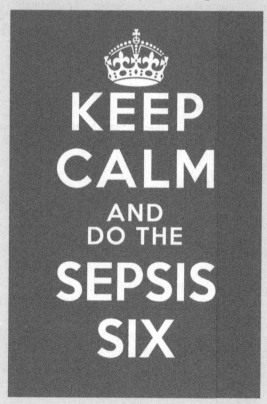

The target behaviour in the first step of the Sepsis Six pathway is to administer oxygen. Summarised in Table 1.2 is who needs to do what, the tools they need, where they need to do it and when they need to do it.

Table 1.2 Behavioural specification of the Sepsis Six pathway

Who	What	Instruments	Where	When
Housekeeper, Porter or Nurse	Put oxygen administration implements in three locations	Nasal specs, fixed performance mask and non-re-breathe mask	a) Sepsis trolley, b) Sepsis grab bag in locked cupboard (keys kept with charge nurse), c) drawers beside beds in Resuscitation Room	Each morning.
Nurse	Check oxygen administration implements in three locations	Nasal specs, fixed performance mask and non-re-breathe mask	a) Sepsis trolley, b) Sepsis grab bag in locked cupboard, c) drawers beside beds in Resuscitation Room	Once a day late morning

Table continued.

Doctor	Prescribe appropriate oxygen saturation and delivery mode Note saturation up to 94-98% for most or 88-92% for patients with respiratory problems. Mode of delivery based on desired flow of inspired O2: nasal spec for up to 24%, fixed performance mask for 20-30% or non-rebreathe mask for up to 80%.	Patient Causality Card (Cas)	With patient, at bedside	Before oxygen is administered
Doctor or Nurse	Circle a) appropriate oxygen saturation and b) delivery mode:	Pathway protocol document	Document kept in folder on Sepsis trolley	Before oxygen is administered
Nurse or Doctor	Administer oxygen	Nasal specs, fixed performance mask or non-re-breathe mask	At bedside	Within one hour of two triggers
Nurse	Record time that oxygen is administered	Pathway protocol document	Document in folder on Sepsis trolley, recorded at bedside	When completed

How to specify the target behaviour - completing Worksheet 3

Worksheet 3 involves you specifying the target behaviour in as much detail as is practicable. Having selected the target behaviour of cleaning hands using alcohol gel in our previous example, we now describe this behaviour in detail (Box 1.7):

Box 1.7 Example of a completed Worksheet 3

Task: Describe the target behaviour according to who needs to do what, when, where, how often and with whom	
Target behaviour	Cleaning hands using alcohol gel
Who **needs to perform the behaviour?**	All hospital staff
What **do they need to do differently to achieve the desired change?**	Clean hands using alcohol gel
When **do they need to do it?**	During each shift
Where **do they need to do it?**	On hospital premises
How often **do they need to do it?**	At the start of each shift After using the toilet Before physical contact with patients After physical contact with patients, visitors or staff members After contact with potentially contaminated materials
With whom **do they need to do it?**	Alone

Now it's your turn!
Please complete Worksheet 3

Step 4: Identify what needs to change

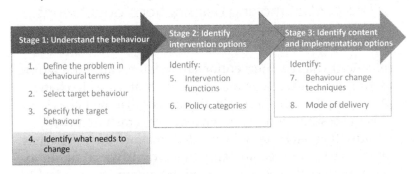

Why identify what needs to change?

Having specified the target behaviour you wish to change, the next step is to identify what needs to change. Specifically we mean identifying what needs to change in the person and/or the environment in order to achieve the desired change in behaviour. Devoting time and effort to fully understanding the target behaviour is a critical and often overlooked step in intervention design. The more accurate this analysis of the target behaviour, the more likely it is that the intervention will change the behaviour in the desired direction.

The cost of making assumptions about what needs to change...

Behaviour change interventions may fail because the wrong assumptions have been made about what needs to change. An example of this from the domain of driving behaviour is the assumption that novice drivers crash frequently because they lack the skills needed to avoid them. This has in the past led to recommendations for drivers thought to be at high risk to be encouraged or sometimes mandated to attend advanced driver courses which it was hoped would mitigate the problem. It turned out that the problem was not so much lack of skill but of motivation. Drivers were motivated to drive in ways that increased the risk of crashing, particularly driving too fast and not paying sufficient care and attention. Therefore, a different kind of intervention was required, one that made novice drivers give a higher priority to driving more slowly and taking more care.

How to identify what needs to change using the COM-B model

COM-B stands for Capability Opportunity Motivation – Behaviour. The COM-B model is the starting point used by the BCW for understanding behaviour in the context in which it occurs. The central tenet of the model is that for any behaviour to occur:

1. there must be the 'capability' to do it: the person or people concerned must have the physical strength, knowledge, skills, stamina etc. to perform the behaviour;
2. there must be the 'opportunity' for the behaviour to occur in terms of a conducive physical and social environment: e.g. it must be physically accessible, affordable, socially acceptable and there must be sufficient time;
3. there must be sufficient strong 'motivation': i.e. they must be more highly motivated to do the behaviour at the relevant time than not to do the behaviour, or to engage in a competing behaviour (Figure 1.4).

Each of these components can be divided heuristically into two types. Capability can be either 'physical' (having the physical skills, strength or stamina) to perform the behaviour or 'psychological' (having the knowledge, psychological skills, strength or stamina) to perform the behaviour. Opportunity can be 'physical' (what the environment allows or facilitates in terms of time, triggers, resources, locations, physical barriers, etc.) or 'social' (including interpersonal influences, social cues and cultural norms). Motivation may be 'reflective' (involving self-conscious planning and evaluations (beliefs about what is good or bad) or 'automatic' (processes involving wants and needs, desires, impulses and reflex responses). These elements of reflective and automatic motivation form the different levels of the human motivational system described in PRIME Theory of Motivation: Plans, Responses, Impulses, Motives (wants and needs) and Evaluations [20].[2]

The COM-B model

Changing the incidence of any behaviour of an individual, group or population involves changing one or more of the following: capability, opportunity, and motivation relating either to the behaviour itself or behaviours that compete with or support it.

[2] More information on PRIME Theory can be found at www.primetheory.com

These components interact as illustrated by the interlinking arrows so that, for example, increasing opportunity or capability can increase motivation. Increased motivation can lead people to do things that will increase their capability or opportunity by changing behaviour. For example, owning a bicycle (opportunity) or being able to ride a bicycle (capability) might increase motivation to ride a bicycle but motivation alone will not improve riding skills or afford access to a bicycle unless the individual acts (behaviour) on this motivation to buy a bike or to practise bicycle riding.

The components can be construed at any level from individual through group through sub-populations and even populations. For example, in an organisation one may wish to characterise an aggregate measure of motivation to engage in a particular behaviour in terms of the mean level or the proportion who report a given level of motivation. Similarly, with capability. Table 1.3 provides definitions and examples of the COM-B model components.

Figure 1.4 The COM-B model

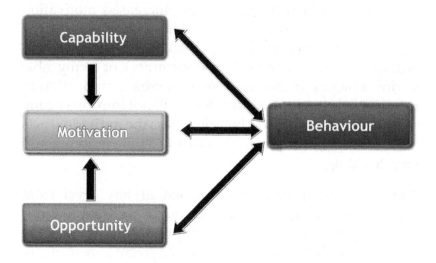

Table 1.3 COM-B model components and examples

COM-B model component Definition	Example
Physical capability Physical skill, strength or stamina	*Having the skill to take a blood sample*
Psychological capability Knowledge or psychological skills, strength or stamina to engage in the necessary mental processes	*Understanding the impact of CO2 on the environment*
Physical opportunity Opportunity afforded by the environment involving time, resources, locations, cues, physical 'affordance'	*Being able to go running because one owns appropriate shoes*
Social opportunity Opportunity afforded by interpersonal influences, social cues and cultural norms that influence the way that we think about things, e.g. the words and concepts that make up our language	*Being able to smoke in the house of someone who smokes but not in the middle of a boardroom meeting*
Reflective motivation Reflective processes involving plans (self-conscious intentions) and evaluations (beliefs about what is good and bad)	*Intending to stop smoking*
Automatic motivation Automatic processes involving emotional reactions, desires (wants and needs), impulses, inhibitions, drive states and reflex responses	*Feeling anticipated pleasure at the prospect of eating a piece of chocolate cake*

It may seem obvious that one should understand the target behaviour before designing the intervention. However, there are many examples of costly interventions that have been designed based on little or no understanding of the behaviour they aim to change which have failed to show an effect or worse, have had the opposite effect than intended. For example:

- DARE (Drug Abuse Resistance Education) programme in US schools: evidence that it was at best ineffective when students were followed up 10 years later [21]. The programme focused on reflective motivation but the anti-drug rhetoric was thought to alienate students. In addition, portraying drug abuse as more frequent than it was may have created a more conducive social environment for taking drugs.

- The UK government's alcohol strategy relies heavily on trying to make people believe that drinking responsibly is a good thing and drinking 'too much' is wrong – thus focusing on reflective motivation – an approach possibly influenced by vested interests and justified by little more than a common-sense analysis of how this kind of behaviour can be changed. Yet the evidence strongly and consistently shows that this approach has been ineffective and that changing opportunity and automatic motivation by raising the price and reducing the times and locations where alcohol can be obtained are effective [22].

- During the 2009 pandemic flu outbreak, the UK government organised a national campaign to immunise health care professionals and high risk sections of the population. Despite major efforts to ensure adequate stocks of immunisation at points of delivery, uptake was low, largely because the motivation amongst target groups was not assessed or addressed and motivation remained low. As noted by Deidre Hine, author of an independent review of the Government's response to the pandemic, 'While the government tracked public opinion and tailored its communications work accordingly, it could have been more proactive in identifying and challenging inaccurate information or advice and responding to concerns and misunderstandings. A more aggressive communications campaign that focused on dispelling concerns that the vaccine was not safe and had been rushed into production without the usual rigorous testing and licensing may have helped uptake rates.' Results from a national weekly tracker survey about H1N1 communications identified a low level of concern about catching swine flu and that the strongest predictor of vaccine uptake was how concerned people were about catching swine flu [23].

The components of COM-B can be further elaborated into 14 domains, using a more detailed tool to understand behaviour, the Theoretical Domains Framework (TDF; see optional Step 4a at the end of this Chapter).

How to identify what needs to change using the COM-B model – completing Worksheet 4

When collecting information to understand the target behaviour, data should be collected from as many relevant sources as possible as the most accurate picture will be informed by multiple perspectives. In a healthcare setting this might be frontline staff who perform the target behaviour, managers, patients, or other 'stakeholders'. It is well established that often we have poor insight into why we behave as we do (Nisbett and Wilson, 1977) so triangulating data using multiple sources will strengthen our understanding of behaviour. If possible, therefore, intervention designers should also collect data using a variety of methods, including interviews and focus groups, questionnaires, direct observation, review of relevant local documents such as service protocols and expert opinion. If a consistent picture of a behaviour and the factors influencing it is obtained from more than one source and using more than one method, it increases confidence in the analysis. However, the nature of the behaviour may constrain the method of data collection; for example, observation is obviously unlikely to be feasible if the behaviour occurs infrequently or privately as occurs behind screens in hospital wards.

Collecting information by interview or focus group

In conducting interviews or focus groups, designers are advised to:

- Ask open-ended questions to promote exploration of ideas rather than yes/no responses;

- Be cautious when asking direct questions about influences on current behaviour because of social desirability and professional identity biases;

- Ask questions in relation to specific instances of current or recent behaviour and in relation to specific contexts (where and when). The third column of Table 1.2 provides examples of questions to ask to assess components of the COM-B model. Designers are encouraged to adapt these to the behaviours and contexts they are targeting.

Collecting information by questionnaire

Self-evaluation by questionnaire is a potentially useful source of information. It will be useful to the extent that respondents have insight into what it would take for them to change their behaviour and were willing to respond honestly. A preliminary version of the COM-B Self-Evaluation Questionnaire (COM-B-Qv1) is below in Box 1.8. At the time of writing it has yet to be evaluated. It may be better in some cases to use it as a basis for designing a questionnaire that addresses the behaviour more specifically. The important thing is to ensure that the full range of possible factors are addressed in a way that can elicit relevant ideas from respondents.

Box 1.8 COM-B Self-Evaluation Questionnaire (COM-B-Qv1)

When it comes to you personally [doing or not doing x; e.g. stopping smoking], what do you think it would take for you to do it? (Circle any of the items on the list that you think apply; you can circle as many or as few as you think appropriate. Some of the items may look strange, but that is just because we need to include anything that might possibly apply for some people.)

In each case please would you say why you think it might be important for you.

I would have to ...

Capability

1.	know more about why it was important	e.g. have a better understanding of the benefits of stopping smoking
2.	know more about how to do it	e.g. have a better understanding of effective ways to lose weight
3.	have better physical skills	e.g. learn how to operate machinery more effectively in one's job
4.	have better mental skills	e.g. learn how to reason more effectively
5.	have more physical strength	e.g. build up muscles for demanding physical work
6.	have more mental strength	e.g. develop stronger resilience against cravings
7.	overcome physical limitations	e.g. get around problems of stature or disability
8.	overcome mental obstacles	e.g. reduce unwanted urges or feelings
9.	have more physical stamina	e.g. develop greater capacity to maintain physical effort
10.	have more mental stamina	e.g. develop greater capacity to maintain mental effort

Opportunity

11.	have more time to do it	e.g. create dedicated time during the day
12.	have more money	e.g. be given or earn funds to support the behaviour
13.	have the necessary materials	e.g. acquire better tools for the job
14.	have it more easily accessible	e.g. provide easier access to facilities
15.	have more people around them doing it	e.g. be part of a 'crowd' who are doing it
16.	have more triggers to prompt them	e.g. have more reminders at strategic times
17.	have more support from others	e.g. have one's family or friends behind one

Motivation

18.	feel that you want to do it enough	e.g. feel more of a sense of pleasure or satisfaction from doing it
19.	feel that you need to do it enough	e.g. care more about the negative consequences of not doing it
20.	believe that it would be a good thing to do	e.g. have a stronger sense that one should do it
21.	develop better plans for doing it	e.g. have clearer and better developed plans for achieving it
22.	develop a habit of doing it	e.g. get into a pattern of doing it without having to think
23.	something else (please specify)	

Recording the behavioural diagnosis
Items from the COM-B-Q can also be used to structure wider information gathering to undertake a behavioural diagnosis as in the COM-B Behavioural Diagnosis Form (COM-B-D) (Box 1.9). This may include evidence from randomized controlled trials, interviews, literature reviews, and theoretical analysis. The sources should be stated.

Box 1.9 COM-B Behavioural Diagnosis Form (COM-B-D)

When it comes to an individual/group/population [doing or not doing x; e.g. stopping smoking], use evidence and theory to form a judgement about which of the following needs to change and in each case whether it should be targeted directly or through one of the other elements of the COM-B system.

Note that it may be appropriate to apply this analysis to one or more supportive or competing behaviours.
The individual/group/population would have to ...

Capability

1.	know more about why it was important	e.g. have a better understanding of the benefits of stopping smoking
2.	know more about how to do it	e.g. have a better understanding of effective ways to lose weight
3.	have better physical skills	e.g. learn how to operate machinery more effectively in one's job
4.	have better mental skills	e.g. learn how to reason more effectively
5.	have more physical strength	e.g. build up muscles for demanding physical work
6.	have more mental strength	e.g. develop stronger resilience against cravings
7.	overcome physical limitations	e.g. get around problems of stature or disability

8.	overcome mental obstacles	e.g. reduce unwanted urges or feelings
9.	have more physical stamina	e.g. develop greater capacity to maintain physical effort
10.	have more mental stamina	e.g. develop greater capacity to maintain mental effort

Opportunity

11.	have more time to do it	e.g. create dedicated time during the day
12.	have more money	e.g. be given or earn funds to support the behaviour
13.	have the necessary materials	e.g. acquire better tools for the job
14.	have it more easily accessible	e.g. provide easier access to facilities
15.	have more people around them doing it	e.g. be part of a 'crowd' who are doing it
16.	have more triggers to prompt them	e.g. have more reminders at strategic times
17.	have more support from others	e.g. have one's family or friends behind one

Motivation

18.	feel that they want to do it enough	e.g. feel more of a sense of pleasure or satisfaction from doing it
19.	feel that they need to do it enough	e.g. care more about the negative consequences of not doing it
20.	believe that it would be a good thing to do	e.g. have a stronger sense that one should do it
21.	develop better plans for doing it	e.g. have clearer and better developed plans for achieving it
22.	develop a habit of doing it	e.g. get into a pattern of doing it without having to think
23.	something else (please specify)	

But I do not have the time or resources!

It may be that you don't have sufficient time or resources to collect data using methods such as experiments, surveys, interviews or focus groups and so you might need to adapt your methods. For example, one option requiring fewer resources and less time would be to conduct a structured discussion with stakeholders, or even just the staff team, based on the COM-B model components and/or domains in the TDF.

Consideration of competing behaviours

In analysing the target behaviour it is important to remember the system within which the behaviour sits and consider alternative behaviours or goals that may be in competition with the target behaviour. For example, in the moment at which hand hygiene behaviours should be performed there are likely to be competing demands on the staff member. Reducing these demands or establishing procedures for these to be performed more efficiently will help achieve the target behaviour. Considering behaviours together as a system leads one not only to promote behaviours that support the desired behaviour but also to inhibit behaviours that compete with the desired behaviour. Bringing about changes in competing or facilitating behaviours will also be helped by analysing these behaviours in terms of COM-B.

While we have discussed promoting desired behaviours, the same approach can be used to decrease undesired behaviours. For example, promoting smoking cessation involves reducing both reflective and automatic motivation to reduce or cease the behaviour and promoting behaviours such as medication adherence and use of, for example, UK's NHS Stop Smoking Services that will assist with this.

Worksheet 4 (Box 1.10) guides the completion of a 'behavioural analysis' of what needs to change in order to make the target behaviour more likely to occur. This is based on the example of disinfecting hands using alcohol gel.

Box 1.10 Example of a completed Worksheet 4

Task: Use the COM-B model to identify what needs to change in order for hospital staff to disinfect their hands using alcohol gel in identified high risk situations:

COM-B components	What needs to happen for the target behaviour to occur?	Is there a need for change?
Physical capability	Have the physical skills to clean hands	No change needed as hospital staff have these skills
Psychological capability	Know the correct technique to clean hands	No change needed as knowledge of hand cleaning techniques is sufficient
	Know how to create 'if-then' rules to prompt hand cleaning	Change needed as hospital staff do not necessarily know how to create and routinely apply if-then rules
Physical opportunity	Have alcohol gel available	No change needed as gel is available at each bedside
Social opportunity	See senior health professionals clean their hands using alcohol gel	Change needed as staff do not always see seeing senior health professionals cleaning their hands using alcohol gel
Reflective motivation	Hold beliefs that using alcohol gel more frequently will reduce infection transmission	No change needed as research literature shows staff hold these beliefs
	Believing that consistent hand hygiene will require improved cognitive and self-regulation skills	Change needed as staff do not necessarily recognise the value of these skills
Automatic motivation	Have established routines and habits for hand cleaning	Change needed to establish routine and habit formation
Behavioural diagnosis of the relevant COM-B components:	Psychological capability, social opportunity, reflective and automatic motivation need to change in order for the target behaviour	

74

Now it's your turn!
Please complete Worksheet 4

Case study examples of using the COM-B model to identify what needs to change

Case studies in Boxes 1.11-1.14 show how the COM-B model has been used to (i) understand why GPs use different strategies to assess cardiovascular disease risk, (ii) develop a conceptual model to understand non-adherence to cystic fibrosis treatment, (iii) analyse eating behaviours as part of the design of weight management smartphone applications, (iv) analyse GPs' use of 'fit notes' for patients to inform guidance and Government policy.

The COM-B model has been used to identify what it takes to change health professional behaviour (Box 1.11).

Box 1.11 Using the COM-B model to identify targets for interventions

General practitioners' use of different assessment strategies for cardiovascular disease risk [24]

Background: Guidelines for cardiovascular disease (CVD) prevention suggest that absolute risk (AR) assessment should be used to guide risk-reducing interventions. A number of AR models have been developed. Among these, the Framingham Risk Score (which estimates the risk of heart attack within 10 years) is recommended in Australian evidence-based guidelines on CVD risk reduction.

Aim: To identify factors that influence general practitioners' use of absolute risk (AR) in cardiovascular disease (CVD) risk assessment.

Method: Twenty five GPs working in New South Wales, Australia, participated in semi-structured interviews. The COM-B model was used to identify targets for interventions to promote GPs' use of AR assessment.

Results: Five different categories of AR use were identified. The authors categorised reasons for selecting these strategies into GP and patient factors and coded them using the COM-B model (Table 1.4):

Box continued.

Table 1.4 Reasons for using AR strategy coded using COM-B

Strategy	Description	GP Factors	Patient Factors	Targets to Improve GP use of AR
AR focused	AR used when considered useful and appropriate for patient	1.Sees following guidelines as important 2.Is familiar with AR model and calculation tools 3.Trusts AR as objective and evidence-based, and helpful for clinical decision-making	1.Patient is borderline for medical treatment, and AR assists in decision-making 2.Patient has no additional risk factors 3.Patient has requested a general health check 4.Patient is interested in seeing evidence for treatment decisions 5.Patient is high risk but resistant, and needs motivation 6.Patient is low risk but concerned, and needs reassurance	Capability: Guidance on the use of the Framingham model versus alternative AR models
AR adjusted	AR adjusted up or down based on presence of additional risk/protective factors	1.Sees following guidelines as important 2.Is familiar with AR model and calculation tools 3.Trusts AR as objective and evidence-based, and helpful for clinical decision-making	1. Patient has additional risk factors that are not specified in AR tools, so risk adjusted upward 2. Patient has a very healthy lifestyle, so adjust risk downwards	Capability: Uncertainty about how to account for risk factors perceived to be outside of the AR model
Clinical judgement	Clinical judgement considered to be as good as or better than AR	1.Belief that clinical judgement takes more risk factors into account 2.Belief in capability to use clinical judgement due to experience	1.Patient is obviously low risk for CVD 2.Patient is obviously high risk for CVD 3. Patient has additional risk factors that are not specified in AR tools	Motivation: Perception that clinical judgement is as good as or better than AR

Passive disregard	AR not used due to lack of time, access to AR calculation tools or experience with AR tools	1.Lack of experience using AR calculation tools 2.Views lack of time and access to AR tools as barriers 3. May acknowledge they should use AR more	1. Patient is used to individual risk factor assessment and so expects it 2. Patient's previous consultations have always been focused on monitoring one isolated risk factor	Opportunity: External barriers to AR assessment. Capability: Poor knowledge of AR model and tools Motivation: focus on individual risk factors out of habit or routine
Active disregard	AR rejected where considered unhelpful or inappropriate for patient	1.Views guidelines as flexible or irrelevant to individual patients 2.Concerned about overservicing patients with unnecessary assessment, and the related costs 3.Views population-based approach as irrelevant to individual patients 4.Focused on patient's agenda for GP appointment 5.More focused on lifestyle risk factors	1.Patient is seen as uninterested in CVD risk 2.Patient has more important health problems than CVD risk 3.Patient is low risk but has lifestyle risk factors, so seeing low AR could demotivate them 4.Patient is low risk but highly anxious, so may be made anxious even by low risk 5.Patient has low literacy so unlikely to understand AR percentage	Opportunity: Patient barriers to AR assessment Motivation: belief that AR is not helpful for individual patients

AR = absolute risk; CVD = cardiovascular disease

Conclusion: Using the COM-B model to categorise reasons for partial or non-use of AR assessment is the first step in designing interventions to promote its use in the assessment of CVD risk

The case study in Box 1.12 illustrates how the COM-B model has been used to extend an existing model of medication adherence making it relevant to a particular context; in this example adherence to cystic fibrosis medication.

Box 1.12 Using the COM-B model to develop a conceptual model to understand non-adherence to cystic fibrosis treatment [25]

Understanding habit formation for cystic fibrosis treatment [25]

Aim: To use the COM-B model to extend a framework of adherence to medication in order to understand how medication-taking habits develop in people with cystic fibrosis.

Method: A framework to explain adherence to medication, the Necessity-Concerns Framework (Horne, 1997[i]), posits that the balance between beliefs about necessity for a prescribed medication and concerns about effects of medication explains the extent to which people adhere to medication. The COM-B model was used to extend this framework to cover capability and opportunity and to consider change over time in order to explain how adherence to nebulisers in the treatment of cystic fibrosis requires habit formation.

Results: A schematic representation of the process of habit formation based on the COM-B model and the Necessity-Concerns Framework is shown below in Figure 1.5. This figure illustrates how the COM-B model components are used to represent the potential barriers to adherence in those who won't ('motivation') and those who can't ('capability' and 'opportunity') adhere and how 'reflective motivation' gives way to 'automatic motivation' over time in those who develop habits.

[i]Horne R (1997) Representations of medication and treatment: Advances in theory and measurement In: Petrie KJ, Weinman JA, editors. Perceptions of Health and Illness: Current Research and Applications. London: Harwood Academic Press. 155–188.

Figure 1.5 Using the COM-B model and Necessity-Concerns Framework to explain habit formation in medication adherence

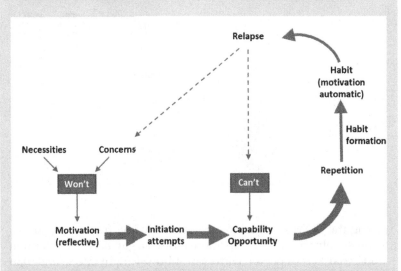

Figure 1.6 illustrates how the components of the COM-B model interact and change over time during the process of habit formation. The increasing size of circles over time shows increasing 'capability' and 'opportunities' as habits are formed. The increasing ratio of 'automatic' to 'reflective motivation' over time depicts the process by which control over behaviour passes from conscious decision-making to routines and environmental triggers which allow behaviour to occur with minimum effort.

Box continued.

Figure 1.6 Interactions between COM-B components during habit formation

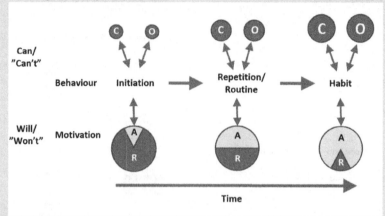

Using the COM-B model to extend an existing framework in this context helps to explain why there is often a gap between intention and behaviour. A person with cystic fibrosis might intend and plan to take their medication but repeatedly fail because of capability or opportunity problems or due to difficulties in establishing a habit. Conducting a behavioural analysis using the COM-B model prompts intervention designers to consider 'capability', 'opportunity' and 'motivation', including building routines and habit formation.

The following case studies (Box 1.13) show how the COM-B can be used to understand behaviour as a first step in developing e-health interventions.

Box 1.13 Using the COM-B model as a starting point for intervention design

Design of a weight management smartphone 'app' for parents of overweight children [26]

Aim: To understand behaviours related to weight management in parents of overweight children as part of the design of a weight management mobile 'app'.

Method: Focus groups were conducted with parents of overweight children who had been referred to a weight management programme. Questions were framed using the COM-B model and parents were asked about what would need to change in order to achieve the following target behaviour: Providing appropriate portion sizes across the five food groups. The focus groups were audio-recorded and transcribed to facilitate the coding of statements using the COM-B model.

Results: The findings revealed shortfalls in capability, opportunity and motivation. Change was identified for 'psychological capability' in that parents reported a lack of knowledge and monitoring of appropriate food portion sizes as well as a difficulty in the comprehension of food packaging portion guidelines and measurements of food portions.

Box continued.

Parents were not confident in their ability to provide correct portion sizes: this was coded as 'reflective motivation'. Parents were also unwilling to read portion and measurement guidelines on food labels due to difficulties understanding them and lack of time, and cited a preference for using household items such as tablespoons and cups as measuring tools instead of scales. This was coded as 'reflective motivation' and 'physical opportunity'. Lastly, partners were not always supportive of efforts to provide appropriate portion sizes and continued to give too big portion sizes: this was coded as 'social opportunity'.

Understanding these target behaviours within the framework of COM-B provides the first steps in selecting appropriate intervention strategies to bring about the desired change.

Development of a smart phone-based attentive eating intervention [27]

Aim: To understand attentive eating behaviour in its context as a starting point for intervention design.

Method: The target behaviour was attentive eating which involves recalling earlier food consumed immediately prior to eating. Drivers of this behaviour were identified using the COM-B model.

Results: The following COM-B components were identified as being relevant to the target behaviour:

'Psychological capability': Individuals may lack knowledge of the potentially harmful effects of non-attentive eating and the skills of recording what they have eaten.

'Physical opportunity': Individuals may not have the physical opportunity in terms of the necessary tools to record what they have eaten in order to increase awareness of food already consumed.

'Automatic motivation': Non-attentive eating might occur because the individual is doing so out of habit.

The intervention designers then used the COM-B model to design an intervention suitable delivery as a smartphone app:

'Capability': Storage and relay of eating episodes using smartphone app technology increases capability of achieving key target behaviours. Automated instructions and guidance ensure target behaviours are fully completed without error.

'Opportunity': Smartphones are widely used, which should ensure: 1) Easy access to intervention tool (physical opportunity), 2) Socially acceptable tool (social opportunity). Automated reminders increase the number of appropriate opportunities to complete target behaviour (physical opportunity).

'Motivation': Personalisation of intervention tool and automatic reminders encourage continued use and promote habitual use (automatic motivation). Storage and presentation of information outlines why the intervention tool will be beneficial (reflective motivation).

Conclusion: The intervention designers have demonstrated how the COM-B model's use can be used to analyse behaviour in context as the basis for designing a smartphone app to deliver the intervention.

The COM-B model has been applied retrospectively to identify and describe factors that may be inhibiting policy implementation (Box 1.14).

Box 1.14 Using the COM-B to inform policy implementation

Revising guidance for GPs on using the fit note [28]

SICK NOTE

Aim: To understand behaviours related to GP use of a note recording patients' fitness for work status and to improve GP use of the fit note through revised guidance.

TO

Method: Behaviours relevant to the overall aim of effective use of the fit note were identified through qualitative research. Barriers to and facilitators of each behaviour were identified from the literature and coded into COM-B components. An example is provided here.

FIT NOTE

Results: The behaviour 'use the comments section every time an individual has been assessed as may be fit for work' was targeted for change. Barriers to this behaviour identified from the literature included (i) lack of information about what to write in this section which was coded as 'psychological capability' and (ii) expectation that the employer will read, value and where possible act upon GP advice which was coded as 'reflective motivation'.

Conclusion: Applying the COM-B model in this way provided a framework for identifying difficulties with completing the fit note as a step towards improving policy implementation and revising guidelines.

Optional Step 4a: Identify what needs to change using the Theoretical Domains Framework (TDF)

The Theoretical Domains Framework (TDF; [10, 29]) was developed in response to requests from implementation researchers who recognised that implementation of evidence-based practice depends on changing behaviour and theories of behaviour change are therefore very relevant and potentially helpful in informing implementation interventions. However, they were aware of the large number of such theories and their overlapping constructs and lacked a method for selecting and applying such theories. (A recent cross-disciplinary review has identified 83 theories of behaviour change [30].) There is some indication that theory-based behaviour change interventions are more effective than those which are not [31-36] although the evidence is neither consistent nor strong [37]. The TDF is an integrative framework synthesising key theoretical constructs used in relevant theories[3] and was developed in a collaboration between psychologists and implementation researchers.

The framework consists of 14 domains: knowledge; skills; memory, attention and decision processes; behavioural regulation; social/professional role and identity; beliefs about capabilities; optimism; beliefs about consequences; intentions; goals; reinforcement;

[3]The original TDF [29] was developed by an international panel of 32 experts in behaviour change who identified 128 constructs from 33 behaviour change theories and simplified them into domains. Usability was developed with an international team of implementation scientists. The TDF has been validated and refined by an international panel of 36 experts in behaviour change [10]

87

emotion; environmental context and resources; and social influences. Definitions of these domains and their component constructs are listed in Table 1.5, along with exemplar questions for use in interviews or focus groups to inform the behavioural analysis and the intervention. Questionnaires based on the 12-domain TDF [29] have been developed in the areas of patient safety [38] and physical activity [39]. A generic questionnaire for use in implementation research has also been developed based on the 14-domain TDF [40].

Table 1.5 TDF domain definitions, theoretical constructs and example questions

Domain Definition	Theoretical constructs represented within each domain	Interview questions[c]
Knowledge An awareness of the existence of something	Knowledge (including knowledge of condition / scientific rationale); procedural knowledge; knowledge of task environment	*Do you know about x?*
Skills An ability or proficiency acquired through practice	Skills; skills development; competence; ability; interpersonal skills; practice; skill assessment	*Do you know how to do x?*
Memory, attention and decision Processes The ability to retain information, focus selectively on aspects of the environment and choose between two or more alternatives	Memory; attention; attention control; decision making; cognitive overload / tiredness	*Is x something you usually do?*
Behavioural regulation Anything aimed at managing or changing objectively observed or measured actions	Self-monitoring; breaking habit; action planning	*Do you have systems that you could use for monitoring whether or not you have carried x?*

Social/professional role and identity A coherent set of behaviours and displayed personal qualities of an individual in a social or work setting	Professional identity; professional role; social identity; identity; professional boundaries; professional confidence; group identity; leadership; organisational commitment	*Is doing x compatible or in conflict with professional standards/identity?*
Beliefs about capabilities Acceptance of the truth, reality, or validity about an ability, talent, or facility that a person can put to constructive use	Self-confidence; perceived competence; self-efficacy; perceived behavioural control; beliefs; self-esteem; empowerment; professional confidence	*How difficult or easy is it for you to do x?*
Optimism The confidence that things will happen for the best or that desired goals will be attained	Optimism; pessimism; unrealistic optimism; identity	*How confident are you that the problem of implementing x will be solved?*
Beliefs about consequences Acceptance of the truth, reality, or validity about outcomes of a behaviour in a given situation)	Beliefs; outcome expectancies; characteristics of outcome expectancies; anticipated regret; consequents	*What do you think will happen if you do x?*
Intentions A conscious decision to perform a behaviour or a resolve to act in a certain way	Stability of intentions; stages of change model; transtheoretical model and stages of change	*Have they made a decision to do x?*
Goals Mental representations of outcomes or end states that an individual wants to achieve	Goals (distal / proximal) ; goal priority; goal / target setting; goals (autonomous / controlled); action planning; implementation intention	*How much do they want to do x?*
Reinforcement Increasing the probability of a response by arranging a dependent relationship, or contingency, between the response and a given stimulus	Rewards (proximal / distal, valued / not valued, probable / improbable); incentives; punishment; consequents; reinforcement; contingencies; sanctions	*Are there incentives to do x?*

Table continued.

Emotion A complex reaction pattern, involving experiential, behavioural, and physiological elements, by which the individual attempts to deal with a personally significant matter or event	Fear; anxiety; affect; stress; depression; positive / negative affect; burn-out	*Does doing x evoke an emotional response?*
Environmental context and resources Any circumstance of a person's situation or environment that discourages or encourages the development of skills and abilities, independence, social competence, and adaptive behaviour	Environmental stressors ; resources / material resources ; organisational culture / climate ; salient events / critical incidents; person x environment interaction; barriers and facilitators	*To what extent do physical or resource factors facilitate or hinder x?*
Social influences Those interpersonal processes that can cause individuals to change their thoughts, feelings, or behaviours	Social pressure; social norms; group conformity; social comparisons; group norms; social support; power; intergroup conflict; alienation; group identity; modelling	*To what extent do social influences facilitate or hinder x?*

[c] Summarised from Michie et al. (2005)

A large number of studies have used the TDF to assess implementation problems and design interventions to improve implementation of evidence-based practice in a variety of health settings [41]. These include: smoking cessation by midwives [42] and dental providers [43]; acute low back pain in primary care [44]; transfusion prescribing [45]; hand hygiene [46]; mental health [47]; GP prescribing for upper-respiratory tract infections [48]. The TDF has been used primarily in the context of health to understand behaviour at the individual level, but it can also be used in a variety of contexts to understand behaviour at the organizational and community level and to identify external factors influencing behaviours. These include the physical environment and organizational factors. If it is not feasible to assess all 14 domains, COM-B analysis can be used as a screening tool to give an indication of which domains to select in conducting more detailed diagnostic interviews.

Each domain of the TDF relates to a COM-B component. Figure 1.7 illustrates how domains of the TDF link to each COM-B component.

Figure 1.7 TDF domains linked to COM-B components

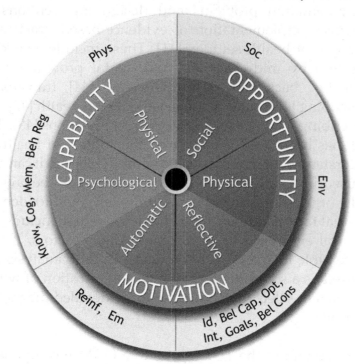

Sources of behaviour

TDF Domains

Soc - Social influences
Env - Environmental Context and Resources
Id - Social/Professional Role and Identity
Bel Cap - Beliefs about Capabilities
Opt - Optimism
Int - Intentions
Goals - Goals
Bel Cons - Beliefs about Consequences
Reinf - Reinforcement
Em - Emotion
Know - Knowledge
Cog - Cognitive and interpersonal skills
Mem - Memory, Attention and Decision Processes
Beh Reg - Behavioural Regulation
Phys - Physical skills

We encourage designers to read the paper 'Developing theory-informed behaviour change interventions to implement evidence into practice' [44] which describes how to collect and analyse data using the Theoretical Domains Framework. It is published in the open access journal, Implementation Science.

How to identify what needs to change using the TDF - completing Worksheet 4a

If a more detailed understanding of the behaviour is required, you can use the TDF to expand on COM-B components identified in the behavioural diagnosis. This is illustrated in Box 1.5 in relation to the target behaviour of cleaning hands.

Box 1.15 Example of a completed Worksheet 4a
Task: Use the TDF to expand on COM-B components
identified in the behavioural diagnosis.

Task: Use the TDF to expand on COM-B components identified in the behavioural diagnosis.

COM-B component identified in the behavioural analysis	Domains linking to COM-B component	Relevance of domain
Psychological capability	Knowledge	Know how to create and apply 'if-then' rules to prompt hand cleaning
	Cognitive and interpersonal skills	Not relevant to hand cleaning
	Memory attention and decision processes	Notice and remember to wash hands
	Behavioural regulation	Develop skills of goal setting, self-monitoring and applying 'if-then' rules
Social opportunity	Social influences	The opportunity to observe senior health professionals clean their hands using alcohol gel
Reflective motivation	Social professional role and identity	Not relevant - hand cleaning is already part of identity
	Beliefs about capabilities	Believing that consistent hand hygiene will require improved cognitive and self-regulation skills
	Optimism	Not relevant
	Intentions	Not relevant – staff intend to keep hands clean
	Goals	Not relevant – as above
	Beliefs about consequences	Not relevant – staff already believe that cleaning hands will reduce infection transmission
Automatic motivation	Reinforcement	Reinforce routines and habits
	Emotion	Not relevant

Now it's your turn!
Please complete Worksheet 4a

Case study examples of different applications of the TDF

The case study in Box 1.16 gives an example of how the TDF has been used to understand the barriers and facilitators of implementing an intervention.

Box 1.16 Using the TDF to understand an implementation problem

Developing theory-informed behaviour change interventions to implement evidence into practice: a systematic approach using the Theoretical Domains Framework [44]

Aim: To understand barriers and facilitators to the uptake of evidence-based guidelines for the management of acute non-specific low back pain in primary care.

Method: Focus groups with 42 GPs considered two target behaviours:
1. Restrict the ordering of plain film x-rays to situations in which fracture is suspected because plain film x-rays are rarely helpful in the management of acute low back pain and are potentially harmful.
2. Advise patients with acute non-specific low back pain to remain active because this reduces pain and disability.

Questions covering each of the domains of the TDF were asked about these target behaviours.

Results: When asked about restricting the ordering of x-rays, GPs felt they did not have the communication skills to reassure concerned patients about not being given an x-ray; this was coded as 'skills'. GPs were also concerned that the consequences of not undertaking an x-ray of a patient with low back pain might result in missing an underlying pathology; this was coded as 'beliefs about consequences'. GPs thought that other health professionals would expect them to order an x-ray; this was coded as 'social influences'. For the second target behaviour, GPs said they often forgot to advise patients to stay active; this was coded as 'memory'. GPs perceived a lack of time for explaining to patients why an x-ray was not needed and for advising them to stay active; this was coded as 'environmental context and resources'.

Having identified domains of the TDF relevant to performing these two behaviours, the research team selected relevant BCTs. This was informed by expert consensus as to which BCTs are likely to be effective in bringing about change for given domains [49].

Case studies in Box 1.17 show how the COM-B model and TDF have been combined to understand implementation problems in health and in environmental sustainability.

Box 1.17 Using COM-B and the TDF to understand implementation problems

Identifying factors influencing variation in physician adenoma detection rates for screening colonoscopy exams: A focus group study using the COM-B model and Theoretical Domains Framework [50]

Aim: To understand factors influencing variation in physician adenoma detection rates (ADRs) for screening colonoscopy exams.

Method: Six focus groups with gastroenterologists and endoscopy nurses at 3 different medical centres were conducted.

Results: Limited time was available to conduct focus groups with doctors who perform routine colonoscopies and with nurses who assist in the process. An adaptive interviewing approach was used in which the COM-B components were used as an initial screen to identify which TDF domains were key and should be discussed in more detail; this is helpful where time is limited. If respondents answered yes to one of the three COM-B filter questions (as shown below) they were prompted with further questions from the theoretical domains within that COM-B component.

1. Would physicians be more/less likely to do 'X' if they had greater physical and/or psychological ability?
Suggested prompts (TDF domains):
- Knowledge – do they know what they should do?

- Physical skills – can they physically do it?
- Memory, Attention and Decision Processes – do they remember to do it?
- Behavioural regulation – are there procedures or ways of working that encourage them to do it?

2. Would physicians be more/less likely to do 'X' if aspects of the physical and/or social environment were changed?
Suggested prompts (TDF domains):
- Environmental Context and Resources - what aspects of the environment (physical vs. resource factors) influence whether or not they do it?
- Social Influences - how might views/opinions of others (colleagues, patients, professional groups) influence their decision to do it?

3. Would physicians be more/less likely to do 'X' if they held more positive beliefs or stronger intentions of doing 'X'.
Suggested prompts (TDF domains):
- Professional/Social Role & Identity - do they think it is part of their job to do it?
- Beliefs about Capabilities – are they confident in doing it?
- Optimism – do they think it's something that can be done?
- Beliefs about Consequences – do they think there are any benefits/harms of doing/not doing it?
- Intentions – have they made a decision (not) to do it?
- Goals – is there anything else that they might want to do or achieve that might interfere with them doing it (clearing email inbox etc)?
- Reinforcement – is there anything that might be reinforcing them to do it?
- Emotion – does doing it provoke an emotional response (e.g. feeling uncomfortable at patients crying out during the exam)?

Using this approach meant that all COM-B components and TDF domains were considered in a relatively short space of time.

Box continued.

Primr✿se

Prediction and management of cardiovascular risk
for people with severe mental illnesses

An example from primary care to manage cardiovascular risk in people with severe mental illness [51]

Aim: To change health professional behaviour to deliver an intervention to reduce cardiovascular disease (CVD) risk in people with severe mental illness (SMI)

Method: Focus groups were conducted with relevant primary care staff, service users and other relevant health professionals to identify what would need to change for the following target behaviours to be performed: Identify patients with SMI on practice register; engage patients; screen for CVD risk factors; offer behavioural support/medication/refer on to specialist services; conduct follow-up monitoring of CVD risk and intervention adherence. Responses were coded using COM-B and TDF.

Results: The following are exemplar preliminary findings from the focus groups:

Screening for CVD was not conducted in some cases because of time constraints – this was coded as COM-B 'physical opportunity' and TDF 'environmental context and resources'.

Practice staff were not always aware of relevant services available to SMI patients. This was coded as COM-B 'psychological capability' and TDF 'knowledge'.

Some practice staff felt uncomfortable 'burdening' the patient with management of their physical as well as mental health. This as coded as COM-B 'automatic motivation' and TDF 'emotion.'

Doctors' perceptions of contraception counselling and provision [52]

Aim: To understand behaviours relating to primary care physicians' counselling about and provision of intrauterine and implantable contraception for adolescents.

Method: Behaviours relevant to counselling about and providing intrauterine devices (IUDs) and implantable contraception for adolescent patients were identified through interviews with 28 GPs, paediatricians, and obstetrician-gynaecologists. The interview schedule was based on the selected domains of the TDF [28] 'knowledge'; 'skills'; 'beliefs about capability' (self-efficacy); 'professional role and identity'; 'beliefs about consequences'; 'environmental context and resources' (environmental constraints); 'motivation and goals'; 'memory, attention and decision processes'; 'behavioural regulation'. Interview responses were coded using the COM-B model (identified by the researchers after conducting the interview study).

Results: All components of COM-B apart from automatic motivation were relevant to the target behaviours:

'Psychological capability' was a barrier to IUD counselling and provision. Some physicians were not aware it could be offered to adolescents in general or to adolescents who have not had children. Physicians did not often offer counselling about implantable contraception because of knowledge gaps. 'Physical capability', having the skills to insert an IUD, was identified as a facilitator of IUD counselling provision.

Box continued.

'Social opportunity' influenced provision of contraception in that the contraceptives were more likely to be prescribed in clinics with a culture of supporting adolescent contraception. 'Physical opportunity' such as the availability of IUDs and implantable contraception devices and a clinician to insert the device in the clinics also influenced counselling and provision.

'Reflective motivation' was identified as a target for change in that physicians' perceptions of the benefits and risks of IUD use influenced their practice.

Using the COM-B model to interpret these data is the first step to intervention design. Having conducted the behavioural analysis, the next step is to systematically link relevant COM-B components to intervention functions. This is covered in Step 5.

Establishing a method for evaluating an intervention to promote recycling [53]

Aims: To evaluate the effectiveness of an intervention to increase recycling in a London university.

Methods: An intervention to promote recycling at University College London was implemented in one campus building. The intervention comprised a new, three-bin recycling system: 1) dry recycling such as paper, plastic, and metal); 2) food waste; 3) non-recyclable waste such as polystyrene. New signage alerted building users to the locations of bins and described how they were to be used.

Pre and post implementation data were collected and compared on the following outcomes: waste volume (kg per full time employee); waste profile (ratio of recyclable to non-recyclable waste); and waste contamination (e.g. recyclable waste placed in non-recyclable waste bin).

Where little or no improvement in outcomes was observed, interviews were conducted with a representative sample of building users to investigate why the intervention was not effective. Interview questions were structured by the COM-B model and TDF to identify whether 'capability', 'motivation' and/ or 'opportunity' factors might explain why the new recycling system was not being used as intended; depending on responses, TDF domains within each of these components were also identified.

Results: The resulting interview schedule grouped by COM-B component and theoretical domain are shown below (Table 1.6).

Table 1.6 Adaptive interview schedule based on COM-B and TDF

COM-B	TDF	Questionnaire item
Psychological capability	Memory, attention and decision processes	1. What efforts have you noticed to promote recycling at UCL? 2. When is the last time you remember seeing a news item or having a conversation about recycling?
Reflective motivation	Beliefs about consequences	3. What Do you think about recycling (in this country) in general? - Do you think it is done well? Why? / Why not? - What impact do you think it has? 4. What do you think about recycling at UCL? - Do you think it is done well? Why? / Why not? - How easy do you think it is to recycle? - What impact do you hope or believe it has?

Box continued.

Psychological capability	Knowledge	5. Please tick which of the following you think can be recycled in this building's recycling facilities: Paper Glass Empty aluminium steel cans Hazardous waste Toner cartridges Tea leaves/coffee grounds Leftover food Empty drink cartons Confectionary Cut flowers/plants Empty plastic bottles Food contaminated packaging (e.g. yoghurt pot) Card Recyclables with contaminated food (e.g. sandwich wrapper) Crisp packets Empty plastic/cardboard cups Sweet wrappers Polystyrene
Psychological capability	Knowledge	6. Have you ever used a bin and were unsure of whether it was intended to be used for recycling or general waste? - If yes, why?
Physical opportunity	Environmental context and resources	7. When you needed one, how often have you had access to a recycling bin? (Every time - most of the time - half of the time – rarely - never) 8. When you needed one, how often have you had access to a general waste bin? (All the time - most of the time - half of the time – rarely - never)
Reflective motivation	Identity	9. Do you think of yourself as someone who is: a committed recycler, casual recycler, not bothered either way about recycling? 10. Do you see recycling at UCL as something that you should be personally responsible for?

Reflective motivation	Beliefs about consequences	11. What do you think are the benefits of recycling: - to you personally? - to the workplace? - to the wider community? 12. What do you think are the harms of not recycling?
Reflective motivation	Intention	13. Is recycling something you generally intend to do? - if 'yes' and you don't recycle, what are the reasons? On a scale of 1 – 7 (7 = very), how effortful do you feel it is to recycle your waste on a daily basis in UCL? 14. Have you ever knowingly put recycling into a general waste bin - if yes, why? 15. Have you ever knowingly put general waste in a recycling bin - if yes, why?
Automatic motivation	Reinforcement	16. Would you say that generally you are in the habit of recycling? - if 'no' what would be helpful in developing a routine/habit of recycling?
Reflective motivation	Goals	17. To what extent is recycling a priority for you?
Social opportunity	Social influences	18. Do you think most of your colleagues are committed recyclers, casual recyclers or and not bothered one way or the other? 19. Do you feel you recycle more when other people are around than you do when you are alone? Or the same?

Chapter 2: Identify intervention options

Sometimes, an appropriate behaviour change strategy clearly follows from an existing body of literature and the task is to improve on what is already there or to introduce and evaluate an innovation that looks promising. In the field of smoking cessation, for example, it has been established in multiple randomized controlled trials that brief advice on smoking given opportunistically to patients typically results in some 2% stopping long-term who would not otherwise have done so [54]. A useful next step, then, is to assess what kind of advice gives the best results [55].

Following Steps 1-4 in Chapter 1 you have arrived at a 'behavioural diagnosis' of what needs to change in order for the desired behaviour to occur. In this chapter we will link this behavioural diagnosis with functions that effective intervention are likely to serve and the policy categories through which the intervention could be implemented.

Step 5: Identify intervention functions

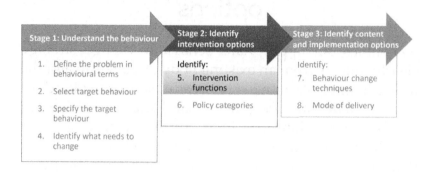

The 'behavioural diagnosis' resulting from the COM-B (or TDF) analysis is a key staging post for designing an intervention. As shown in the case studies in Boxes 1.11-1.14, 1.16-1.17 (pp 76-86, 96-105) the behavioural analysis identifies COM-B components and/or domains of the TDF that can be targeted as potential levers of change.

In 2007, NICE (National Institute for Health and Care Excellence) identified evidence-based principles of behaviour change (summarized in [56]). Below we illustrate how these can be linked with COM-B components.

Maximise **capability** to regulate own behaviour
1. Develop relevant skills such as goal-setting, monitoring and providing feedback
2. Develop specific plans to change

Maximise **opportunity** to support self-regulation
3. Elicit social support
4. Avoid social and other cues for current behaviour
5. Change routines and environment

Increase **motivation** to engage in the desired behaviour
6. Reward change
7. Develop appropriate beliefs, e.g. benefits of changing, others' approval, personal relevance, confidence to change
8. Develop positive feelings about changing
9. Develop new habits

These principles can also be understood in terms of the general functions they serve. By 'intervention function', we mean broad categories of means by which an intervention can change behaviour. In considering possible interventions, it is important to start by considering the full range of possible intervention functions available. This is helped by using a framework of behaviour change to guide intervention design. Many frameworks of behaviour change have been produced, with varying levels of comprehensiveness, coherence and theoretical base. A systematic literature review of frameworks of behaviour change interventions identified 19 frameworks which comprised essentially nine intervention functions and seven policy categories [1]. The resulting integrated framework, the Behaviour Change Wheel (BCW), linked these intervention functions and policy categories to the COM-B model, which forms the hub of the wheel (see Figure 1).

We classify intervention functions rather than interventions because any particular intervention strategy or BCT may have more than one function. For example, a message such as 'Please make sure you use soap when washing your hands - just rinsing them is not enough to kill the bacteria that cause nasty stomach bugs', can serve to improve knowledge but also with words such as 'nasty' it can evoke emotions in a way that goes beyond this into persuasion.

The nine intervention functions identified in synthesising the 19 frameworks are: education, persuasion, incentivisation, coercion, training, restriction, environmental restructuring, modelling and enablement (definitions and examples are given in Table 2.1). If you wish to see the 19 frameworks and the methods used to synthesise them, they are in Appendix 1 and in the supplementary files of the published paper [1].

The BCW does not provide a detailed blueprint for the design of behaviour change interventions, but does provide a systematic and theoretically guided method for identifying the types of interventions and supporting policies that would be expected to be effective for a given behaviour, context and target individual, group or population.

Table 2.1 BCW intervention function definitions and examples

Intervention function	Definition	Example of intervention function
Education	Increasing knowledge or understanding	*Providing information to promote healthy eating*
Persuasion	Using communication to induce positive or negative feelings or stimulate action	*Using imagery to motivate increases in physical activity*
Incentivisation	Creating an expectation of reward	*Using prize draws to induce attempts to stop smoking*
Coercion	Creating an expectation of punishment or cost	*Raising the financial cost to reduce excessive alcohol consumption*
Training	Imparting skills	*Advanced driver training to increase safe driving*
Restriction	Using rules to reduce the opportunity to engage in the target behaviour (or to increase the target behaviour by reducing the opportunity to engage in competing behaviours)	*Prohibiting sales of solvents to people under 18 to reduce use for intoxication*
Environmental restructuring	Changing the physical or social context	*Providing on-screen prompts for GPs to ask about smoking behaviour*

Table continued.

Modelling	Providing an example for people to aspire to or imitate	*Using TV drama scenes involving safe-sex practices to increase condom use*
Enablement	Increasing means/ reducing barriers to increase capability (beyond education and training) or opportunity (beyond environmental restructuring)	*Behavioural support for smoking cessation, medication for cognitive deficits, surgery to reduce obesity, prostheses to promote physical activity*

Linking COM-B and TDF to BCW intervention functions
The COM-B and TDF identify what needs to shift for the desired behaviour to be achieved and therefore what to target in an intervention. The BCW identifies intervention functions and supporting policies likely to be effective in bringing about change. The links between COM-B, TDF and the intervention functions, identified by a group of experts in a consensus exercise are shown in Tables 2.2 and 2.3. For each COM-B component or TDF domain identified as relevant in bringing about the desired change in the target behaviour, Table 2.2 shows which intervention function is likely to be effective in bringing about that change.

Table 2.2 Links between COM-B, TDF and intervention functions

COM-B	TDF	Intervention functions
Physical capability	Physical skills	Training
Psychological capability	Knowledge	Education
	Cognitive and interpersonal skills	Training
	Memory, attention and decision processes	Training Environmental restructuring Enablement
	Behavioural regulation	Education Training Modelling Enablement

Table continued.

Reflective motivation	Professional/social role and identity	Education Persuasion Modelling
	Beliefs about capabilities	Education Persuasion Modelling Enablement
	Optimism	Education Persuasion Modelling Enablement
	Beliefs about consequences	Education Persuasion Modelling
	Intentions	Education Persuasion Incentivisation Coercion Modelling
	Goals	Education Persuasion Incentivisation Coercion Modelling Enablement
Automatic motivation	Reinforcement	Training Incentivisation Coercion Environmental restructuring
	Emotion	Persuasion Incentivisation Coercion Modelling Enablement

Physical opportunity	Environmental context and resources	Training Restriction Environmental restructuring Enablement
Social opportunity	Social influences	Restriction Environmental restructuring Modelling Enablement

Table 2.3 Matrix of links between COM-B and intervention functions

COM-B components	Intervention functions								
	Education	Persuasion	Incentivisation	Coercion	Training	Restriction	Environmental restructuring	Modelling	Enablement
Physical capability					■				■
Psychological capability	■				■				■
Physical opportunity					■		■		■
Social opportunity						■	■	■	■
Automatic motivation		■	■	■			■	■	■
Reflective motivation	■	■	■	■					

Examples of how one could move from COM-B to intervention functions are given in Table 2.4. The constructs in the first column are ways of sub-classifying capability, opportunity and motivation. They provide an intermediate level of abstraction between COM-B and the TDF. Whether these constructs or other are most useful will no doubt depend on the circumstances and the behaviour. At present it is best to think of them as options that can be tried.

Table 2.4 Linking COM-B components to intervention functions

COM-B	Intervention functions
Influencing capability	
Knowledge	**Educate** about ways of enacting the desired behaviour or avoiding the undesired one
Skill	**Train** in cognitive, physical or social skills required for the desired behaviour or avoid the undesired one
Strength	**Train** or **enable** development of mental or physical strength required for the desired behaviour or to resist the undesired one
Stamina/ endurance	**Train** or **enable** endurance required for desired behaviour or sustained resistance to undesired one
Influencing opportunity	
Time	**Train** or **restructure the environment** to reduce time demand or competing time demands for desired behaviour (and additionally use **restriction** to reduce undesired behaviour)

Table continued.

Resources	**Restructure the environment** to increase social support and cultural norms for desired behaviour (and additionally use **restriction** to reduce undesired behaviour)
Location/ physical barriers	**Train** or **Restructure the environment** to provide cues and prompts for desired behaviour (and converse for undesired behaviour)
Interpersonal influences/ cultural expectations	**Restructure the social environment** or use **modelling** to shape people's ways of thinking
Influencing motivation	
Plans	**Educate, train** to form clearer personal rules/ action plans, and train to remember and apply the rules when needed
Evaluations	**Educate** or **persuade** to create more positive beliefs about desired, and negative ones about undesired, behaviour
Motives	**Persuade, incentivise, coerce, model** or **enable** to feel positively about the desired behaviour and negatively about the undesired one
Impulses/ inhibition	**Train** or **enable** to strengthen habitual engagement in the desired behaviour or weaken the undesired one
Responses	**Model** desired behaviour to induce automatic imitation

An example of the way that COM-B categories and intervention functions can be drawn from the field of obesity [57]. Several intervention strategies can be considered to reduce portion size ranging from education to minor environmental restructuring. These strategies are summarized in Table 2.5.

Table 2.5 Linking intervention strategies intervention functions and COM-B components to promote eating smaller food portions

Intervention strategy to reduce portion size	Intervention functions	COM-B
Physical environment		
Increase availability of portion-controlled products	Environmental restructuring	Physical opportunity
Smaller crockery and utensils	Environmental restructuring	Physical opportunity
Food environment		
Clearly signal serving size for large packages	Education	Psychological capability
Decrease portion size of energy dense foods	Environmental restructuring	Physical opportunity

Table continued.

Economic interventions		
Proportional pricing strategies	Coercion	Reflective motivation
Shift balance of promotions from 'super-size' to 'mini-size'	Incentivisation	Reflective motivation
Political interventions		
Mandatory portion caps /supersize bans	Restriction	Physical opportunity

The COM-B model and intervention function matrix (Table 2.3, p116) can also be applied to the research literature to identify potentially useful intervention functions. An example is the provision of preventive anti-retroviral medication (Table 2.6). Although there is good evidence that providing pre-exposure anti-retroviral medication to HIV-negative individuals protects against HIV infection, it is rarely prescribed. Factors militating against this prescribing can be summarised as: health professionals' lack of awareness of preventive anti-retroviral medication [58, 59]; health professionals being unconvinced about the effectiveness of this medication to prevent infection [59-61]; concerns about side-effects [60-63], stigmatisation [59] and cost [59-61]. These can be coded using COM-B and TDF to identify relevant intervention functions to apply to increasing prescribing anti-retroviral medication to HIV-negative individuals (Table 2.6).

Table 2.6 Barriers to preventive anti-retroviral medication prescribing linked to COM-B, TDF and intervention functions

COM-B	Barrier	TDF	Intervention functions
Psychological capability	Knowledge	Lack of awareness of pre-exposure anti-retroviral medication	Education
Reflective motivation	Beliefs about consequences	Lack of conviction about the effectiveness of this medication to prevent infection. Concerns about side-effects and stigmatisation	Education Persuasion Modelling
Physical opportunity	Environmental context and resources	Concerns about cost	Restriction Environmental restructuring Enablement

Using the matrix we can move from understanding the behaviour (prescribing pre-exposure anti-retroviral medication) to selecting intervention functions of education, persuasion, modelling, restriction, environmental restructuring and enablement.

Deciding who to target with the intervention: individual, group or population?

Individual behaviour is influenced by social opportunity in the form of immediate social contacts and wider cultural norms (Figure 2.1). The BCW goes beyond this in recognizing the importance of groups and populations by allowing all the parameters to be specified at group or population level. Thus if you are seeking to change the behaviour of populations, you can specify that behaviour in population terms (e.g. in terms of the proportion who smoke cigarettes, exceed the speed limit on motorways, drink above recommended limits etc.). If you are seeking to change the behaviour of individuals or groups you can specify the behaviour at that level (e.g. increasing the mean number of hours per week spent at the gym). With advances in technology, some of the defining features of 'individual-level' interventions can be applied to whole populations and so the 'individual/population' distinction breaks down.

For example, internet-based interventions that can be accessed by an entire population can be individually tailored and use BCTs that would previously have required human intervention.

Figure 2.1 Individual, community and population-wide influences on health [64]

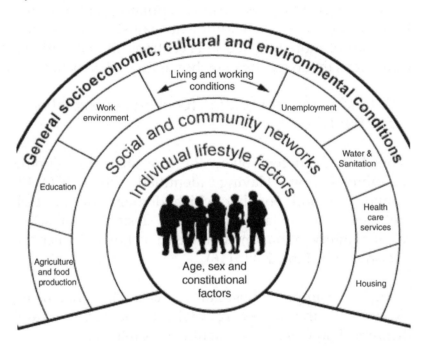

When dealing with populations rather than individuals, it is important to recognise that members of the population will differ in terms of what is required to achieve the target behaviour and many of them will be doing any given behaviour already. This raises issues about whether and how much to target subgroups, and what scope there might be for tailoring to individuals. If tailoring is not possible, then choices have to be made about what intervention strategy will have the greatest aggregate effect while minimising any adverse effects. For example, evidence clearly indicates that raising price and restricting availability reduce excessive alcohol consumption and antisocial behaviours arising from this, including violence and reckless behaviour leading to accidents. However, there is a cost to 'responsible drinkers' and this has hitherto been used as an argument against such measures in favour of more targeted interventions and educational campaigns that have thus far shown little or no benefit.

How to identify intervention functions - completing Worksheet 5

Worksheet 5 guides you in the first step of designing the intervention. Having identified which COM-B components and possibly which domains of the TDF are relevant to the target behaviour, designers can select relevant intervention functions based on links between the two shown in Table 2.3 (p116).

Using the example of hospital staff cleaning hands using alcohol gel the following COM-B components (and theoretical domains) were identified as relevant:

- Psychological capability (knowledge; memory, attention and decision processes, behavioural regulation)
- Social opportunity (social influences)
- Reflective motivation (beliefs about capabilities)
- Automatic motivation (reinforcement)

Tables 2.2 and 2.3 guide the selection of the following candidate intervention functions:

- Education to bring about a change in psychological capability (knowledge);
- Training, environmental restructuring and enablement to bring about a change in psychological capability (memory, attention and decision processes);
- Education, training, modelling and enablement to bring about a change in psychological capability (behavioural regulation)
- Restriction, environmental restructuring, modelling or enablement to bring about change in social opportunity (social influences);
- Education, persuasion, modelling and enablement to bring about a change in reflective motivation (beliefs about capabilities)
- Training, incentivisation, coercion and environmental restructuring to bring about change in automatic motivation (reinforcement).

Be comfortable using judgement

Identifying intervention functions and, as you will see in the next three steps, identifying policy categories, BCTs and mode of delivery requires you to use judgement as to what is most appropriate for the context. The APEASE criteria are suggested to help you make strategic judgements as to what might be most appropriate for the intervention.

We now consider each of the candidate intervention functions using the APEASE criteria (Table 1, p23) to guide our judgement in selecting the most appropriate intervention function (Box 2.1):

Box 2.1 Example of a completed Worksheet 5

Candidate intervention functions	Does the intervention function meet the APEASE criteria (affordability, practicability, effectiveness/cost-effectiveness, acceptability, side-effects/safety, equity) in the context of cleaning hands using alcohol gel?
Education	Not practicable as there is not enough time to take staff off wards to educate them
Persuasion	Unlikely to be effective as most staff intend to clean their hands this intervention function is unlikely to add value
Incentivisation	Yes
Coercion	Not acceptable to staff
Training	Not practicable as there is not enough time to take staff off wards to train them
Restriction	Not practicable as there are no options to restrict in this context
Environmental restructuring	Not practicable to restructure the environment so senior doctors are seen more frequently cleaning their hands to bring about change in social opportunity
Modelling	Not practicable to deliver in this context
Enablement	Yes
Selected intervention functions:	Incentivisation and enablement

Having applied these criteria to consider each candidate intervention function, two are selected, 'incentivisation' and 'enablement'.

Now it's your turn!
Please complete Worksheet 5

If you have access to policy levers

Intervention designers who have access to policy levers should go to Step 6, selecting policy categories, before selecting BCTs and specifying mode of delivery. Designers limited to a specific policy lever are directed to Step 7 to identify BCTs.

Case study examples of using the BCW to design interventions

The BCW can be applied as framework for intervention design in a wide range of contexts. Box 2.2 shows two examples of how the BCW can be used to develop complex, multi-level interventions and tailored interventions.

Box 2.2 Using the BCW to design interventions

Designing complex interventions: Improving Delivery of Paediatric Services in Kenyan Hospitals – The basis for a contextually appropriate intervention strategy and an approach to evaluation [65].

Aim: To promote adherence to evidence-based guidelines for paediatric services in Kenyan hospitals.

Method: Evidence in research literature, and government and hospital reports, were investigated to identify factors influencing the low uptake of evidence-based guidelines for paediatric services at the organisational level (senior and mid-management) and amongst front-line health care professionals. Influential factors were coded according to components of the COM-B model (see Figure 2.2 below) from which appropriate intervention functions of the BCW were selected.

Box continued.

Results: Factors influencing guideline uptake were (i) for senior managers, opportunity in the form of a supportive political environment and appropriate funding and motivation in the form of accountability to staff and institutional reputation, (ii) for mid-managers, having the relevant management skills ('capability') and professional identity ('motivation'), (iii) for front-line staff, having the necessary knowledge of guidelines and skills to carry out recommendations in guidelines ('capability'), having a supportive team and the right physical environment to work in ('opportunity') and perceiving carrying out the recommendations in guidelines as part of their role ('motivation'). From this behavioural analysis the following intervention functions were selected:

- 'Education' (improving knowledge and understanding of roles and responsibilities for key professionals responsible for service provision and improving technical knowledge through a community of practice
- 'Training' (providing key professionals with core skills in management and leadership)
- 'Persuasion' (developing monitoring and evaluation approaches for feedback to hospitals and policy makers on guideline implementation within network hospitals)
- 'Incentivisation' (recognition of achievements within networks and professions)
- 'Environmental restructuring' (promoting reflection on environmental and organisational aspects of service provision)
- 'Modelling' (discussion of identified successful strategies for change within network)
- 'Enablement' (promoting collective action across network to overcome barriers to improving care).

Figure 2.2 Using COM-B to understand multi-level behaviours in a hospital context

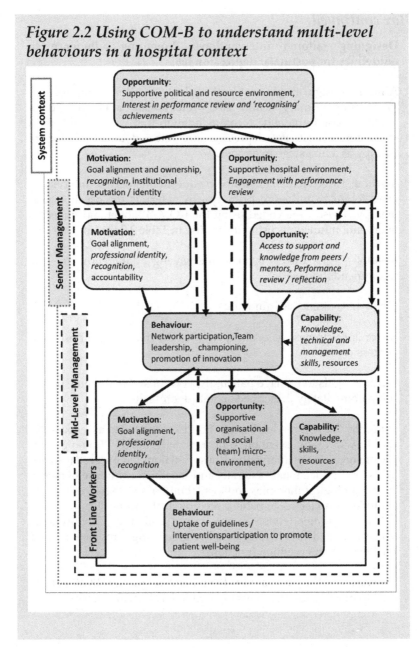

Box continued.

Designing tailored interventions: Promoting adherence to guidelines for post-natal depression [66]

Aim: To design, implement and evaluate a tailored intervention to promote primary health care professionals' adherence to an evidence-based guideline recommendation that women with mild to moderate postnatal depression are referred for psychological therapy as a first stage treatment.

Method: Three factors, identified by questionnaires and interviews, were found to influence primary care referrals for psychological therapy. These were coded using the COM-B model and linked to intervention functions using the matrix in Table 2.3 (p116).

Results: The three factors influencing adherence to the recommendation were:

Factor 1: Awareness of guidelines

Factor 2: Awareness of local expertise in the treatment of post-natal depression

Factor 3: Skills to manage patient expectations of treatment such as being immediately prescribed an anti-depressant

Using the COM-B model, Factors 1 and 2 were coded as 'capability' and linked to intervention functions 'education', 'training' and 'enablement'. In the intervention these functions were served through (i) tailored educational materials and meetings about the evidence for psychological therapies and availability of local services and (ii) reminders on electronic patient records in the form of a summary of the recommendation. Factor 3 was coded as 'opportunity' which is linked to 'environmental restructuring', 'restriction', and 'enablement' intervention functions.

Conclusions: This case study demonstrates how the BCW can be used to develop interventions tailored to local circumstances.

Test your knowledge of intervention functions with the Spin the Wheel Quiz!

Which intervention functions do you think the following are examples of (answers in Appendix 3)?

1. Providing information on benefits of physical activity.
2. Fines for the possession of solvents.
3. Creating a rewards system for GPs who ask about smoking behaviour.
4. Telling drinkers if they drink to excess they will be viewed negatively by their peers.
5. A lecture about safe driving.
6. Using TV advert to encourage condom use.
7. Providing cooking lessons.
8. Supporting GPs to recognise the symptoms ovarian cancer with an information pamphlet.
9. Using positive images of non-smokers to encourage smokers to quit.

Step 6: Identify policy categories

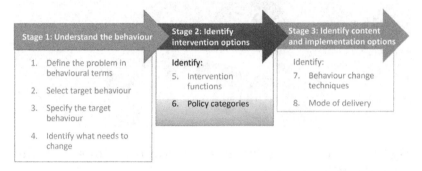

The next step in developing an intervention strategy is to consider what policies would support the delivery of the intervention functions identified in Step 5. In synthesising the 19 frameworks, seven policy categories were identified, representing types of decisions made by authorities that help to support and enact the interventions: 'Communication/marketing' (using print, electronic, telephonic or broadcast media); 'guidelines' (creating documents that recommend or mandate practice, this includes all changes to service provision); 'fiscal' (using the tax system to reduce or increase the financial cost); 'regulation' (establishing rules or principles of behaviour or practice); 'legislation' (making or changing laws); 'environmental/social planning' (designing and/or controlling the physical or social environment); 'service provision' (delivering a service) (definitions and examples are given in Table 2.7).

Table 2.7 BCW policy categories

Policy Category	Definition	Example
Communication/ marketing	Using print, electronic, telephonic or broadcast media	Conducting mass media campaigns
Guidelines	Creating documents that recommend or mandate practice. This includes all changes to service provision	Producing and disseminating treatment protocols
Fiscal measures	Using the tax system to reduce or increase the financial cost	Increasing duty or increasing anti-smuggling activities
Regulation	Establishing rules or principles of behaviour or practice	Establishing voluntary agreements on advertising
Legislation	Making or changing laws	Prohibiting sale or use
Environmental/ social planning	Designing and/ or controlling the physical or social environment	Using town planning
Service provision	Delivering a service	Establishing support services in workplaces, communities etc.

How to identify policy categories

The BCW suggests which policy categories are likely to be appropriate and effective in supporting each intervention function (Tables 2.8 and 2.9).

Table 2.8 Linking BCW intervention functions to policy categories

Intervention function	Policy categories that could deliver intervention functions
Education	Communication/marketing Guidelines Regulation Legislation Service provision
Persuasion	Communication/marketing Guidelines Regulation Legislation Service provision
Incentivisation	Communication/marketing Guidelines Fiscal measures Regulation Legislation Service provision
Coercion	Communication/marketing Guidelines Fiscal measures Regulation Legislation Service provision

Training	Guidelines Fiscal measures Regulation Legislation Service provision
Restriction	Guidelines Regulation Legislation
Environmental restructuring	Guidelines Fiscal measures Regulation Legislation Environmental/social planning
Modelling	Communication/marketing Service provision
Enablement	Guidelines Fiscal measures Regulation Legislation Environmental/social planning Service provision

Table 2.9 Matrix of links between intervention functions and policy categories

In the matrix below, a shaded cell (✓) indicates a link between the policy category and the intervention function.

Policy Categories	Intervention functions								
	Education	Persuasion	Incentivisation	Coercion	Training	Restriction	Environmental restructuring	Modelling	Enablement
Communication/ marketing	✓	✓	✓		✓	✓	✓	✓	
Guidelines	✓	✓	✓	✓	✓	✓	✓		✓
Fiscal measures		✓	✓	✓	✓		✓	✓	✓
Regulation	✓	✓	✓	✓	✓	✓	✓		✓
Legislation	✓	✓	✓	✓	✓	✓	✓		✓
Environ./ Social planning							✓		
Service provision	✓	✓	✓	✓	✓		✓		✓

Having identified the potential policy categories to use, they can be considered using the APEASE criteria set out in Table 1 (p23). In terms of considering evidence, it would be reasonable to give greatest weight to high quality field experiments in the target population concerned addressing the behaviour in question, if available. One should give progressively less weight to studies with lower degrees of experimental control, weaker outcome measures, smaller sample sizes, populations that differ from the target population, contexts that differ from the one in question and behaviours that differ from the target behaviour.

How to identify policy categories – completing Worksheet 6

Continuing the example of cleaning hands using alcohol gel, we have identified the functions that the intervention should serve. The next step is to consider the policy categories that might support the delivery of the intervention functions; in this case, incentivisation and enablement have been selected as the most appropriate based on consideration of the APEASE (Table 1, p23) (Table 2.10).

Table 2.10 Example of a completed Worksheet 6

Intervention function	COM-B component	Potentially useful policy categories	Does the policy category meet the APEASE criteria (affordability, practicability, effectiveness/ cost-effectiveness, acceptability, side-effects/safety, equity) in the context of cleaning hands using alcohol gel?
Incentivisation	Reflective motivation Automatic motivation	Communication/ marketing	Yes
		Guidelines	Unlikely to be effective (add value) as guidelines around hand hygiene already exist
		Fiscal measures	Not relevant in the hospital context
		Regulation	Possible in the long term but not present
		Legislation	Not practicable in the hospital context
		Service provision	Yes
Enablement	Psychological capability Social opportunity Automatic motivation	Guidelines	As above
		Fiscal measures	As above
		Regulation	As above
		Legislation	As above
		Environmental/ social planning	Not practicable in this context
		Service provision	Yes
Policy category selected: Communication/marketing and service provision			

Now it's your turn!
Please complete Worksheet 6

Case study example of using the BCW to describe policy and guidelines

Box 2.3 shows how the BCW can be used to describe policy and guideline content.

Box 2.3 Using the BCW to describe intervention functions and policy categories in the English Tobacco Control Strategy and NICE Guidance on Obesity [1]

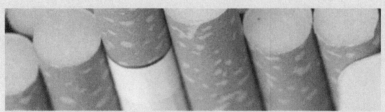

Aim: To test the extent to which intervention functions and policy categories can be used to describe the function and delivery of recommendations for good practice.

Method: The architects of the BCW, Professors Susan Michie and Robert West, independently coded 24 components in the 2010 English Tobacco Control Strategy [67] and 21 components in NICE Guidance on Obesity [68] into intervention functions and policy categories. For example, in the 2010 English Tobacco Control Strategy the recommendation 'remove tobacco products from display in shops' was coded as serving the intervention function 'environmental restructuring' and the policy category 'legislation'.

The level of agreement between coders was calculated and differences were resolved. A second set of coders, the Policy Lead for implementation of the 2010 English Tobacco Control Strategy and a tobacco researcher independently coded the 24 components in the 2010 English Tobacco Control Strategy.

Results: There was good agreement allowing this approach to reliably describe the functions and policy categories of these two national strategies and guidelines. Initial coding of the intervention functions and policy categories resulted in 88% agreement for the 24 components in the 2010 English Tobacco Control Strategy and 79% agreement for the 21 components in the NICE Obesity Guidance. The second coding of the 24 components in the 2010 English Tobacco Control Strategy resulted in 85% agreement with this consensus and Policy Lead and 75% agreement between the consensus and the tobacco researcher.

This illustrates the application of the BCW as a useful tool to describe recommendations in policy documents and evidence-based guidelines.

Chapter 3: Identify content and implementation options

Having identified the intervention functions and policy categories, the next step is to identify intervention content in terms of which BCTs best serve intervention functions and which mode of delivery is appropriate to implement the intervention. This chapter will guide you in the use of evidence and practical factors when identifying BCTs and mode of delivery.

Step 7: Identify behaviour change techniques (BCTs)

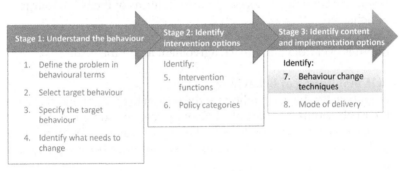

Stage 1: Understand the behaviour	Stage 2: Identify intervention options	Stage 3: Identify content and implementation options
1. Define the problem in behavioural terms 2. Select target behaviour 3. Specify the target behaviour 4. Identify what needs to change	Identify: 5. Intervention functions 6. Policy categories	Identify: 7. Behaviour change techniques 8. Mode of delivery

We are now concerned with identifying which BCTs can deliver the identified intervention functions under the relevant policy categories. A BCT is defined as "an active component of an intervention designed to change behaviour". The defining characteristics of a BCT are that it is observable, replicable, an irreducible component of an intervention designed to change behaviour and a postulated active ingredient within the intervention. It is thus the smallest component compatible with retaining the postulated active ingredients, i.e. the proposed mechanisms of change, and can be used alone or in combination with other BCTs" [69]. Box 3.1 gives three examples of BCTs with their definitions and examples taken from BCTTv1.

Box 3.1 Examples of BCTs in BCTTv1

Habit formation
Definition: Prompt rehearsal and repetition of the behaviour in the same context repeatedly so that the context elicits the behaviour.
Example: Prompt patients to take their statin tablet before brushing their teeth every evening.

Goal setting (behaviour)
Definition: Set or agree a goal defined in terms of the behaviour to be achieved.
Example: Agree a daily walking goal (e.g. to walk for at least 30 minutes every day) and reach agreement about the goal.

Self-monitoring of behaviour
Definition: Establish a method for the person to monitor and record their behaviour(s) as part of a behaviour change strategy.
Example: Ask the person to record daily, in a diary, whether they had brushed their teeth for at least two minutes before going to bed.

The BCT Taxonomy (v1) - a standardised language for describing the active ingredients in interventions

BCTs have been identified in relation to particular types of behaviour such as physical activity, healthy eating, condom use, smoking, excessive alcohol use, professional practice and medication use [3-9, 70]. These behaviour-specific 'taxonomies' of BCTs have been synthesised and refined in an internationally supported piece of work to produce BCT Taxonomy v1, with 93 BCTs. Because 93 items are too many to keep in mind, they were organised into 16 groupings by experts using a 'card sort' technique [2] (see www.ucl.ac.uk/health-psychology/BCTtaxonomy/). The BCT labels within their groupings are shown below, along with full information about one BCT as an illustration (Tables 3.1 and 3.2). The full taxonomy with definitions and examples is given in Appendix 4[4].

---

[4] An interactive online resource is being developed which will provide training for new users of the taxonomy, 'top-up' or 'refresh' training and will continue to support those who have already completed training to use BCTTv1. The site will be accessible from the current BCT Taxonomy project website (http://www.ucl.ac.uk/health-psychology/BCTtaxonomy/). A BCTTv1 smartphone app is also being developed and will be available for android smartphones and iPhones. Links to download sites will be posted on BCT Taxonomy project website.

Table 3.1 Labels of the BCTs within the taxonomy (each has a definition)

Grouping and BCTs	Grouping and BCTs	Grouping and BCTs
1. Goals and planning	**6. Comparison of behaviour**	**12. Antecedents**
1.1. Goal setting (behaviour)	6.1. Demonstration of the behaviour	12.1. Restructuring the physical environment
1.2. Problem solving	6.2. Social comparison	12.2. Restructuring the social environment
1.3. Goal setting (outcome)	6.3. Information about others' approval	12.3. Avoidance/reducing exposure to cues for the behaviour
1.4. Action planning		
1.5. Review behaviour goal(s)	**7. Associations**	12.4. Distraction
1.6. Discrepancy between current behaviour and goal	7.1. Prompts/cues	12.5. Adding objects to the environment
1.7. Review outcome goal(s)	7.2. Cue signalling reward	12.6. Body changes
1.8. Behavioural contract	7.3. Reduce prompts/cues	
1.9. Commitment	7.4. Remove access to the reward	**13. Identity**
	7.5. Remove aversive stimulus	13.1. Identification of self as role model
2. Feedback and monitoring	7.6. Satiation	13.2. Framing/reframing
2.1. Monitoring of behaviour by others without feedback	7.7. Exposure	13.3. Incompatible beliefs
	7.8. Associative learning	13.4. Valued self-identify
2.2. Feedback on behaviour		13.5 Identity associated with changed behaviour
2.3. Self-monitoring of behaiour	**8. Repetition and substitution**	
2.4. Self-monitoring of outcome(s) of behaviour	8.1. Behavioural practice/rehearsal	**14. Scheduled consequences**
2.5. Monitoring of outcome(s) of behaviour without feedback	8.2. Behaviour substitution	14.1. Behaviour cost
	8.3. Habit formation	14.2. Punishment
	8.4. Habit reversal	14.3. Remove reward
2.6. Biofeedback	8.5. Overcorrection	14.4. Reward approximation
2.7. Feedback on outcome(s) of behaviour	8.6. Generalisation of target behaviour	14.5. Rewarding completion
	8.7. Graded tasks	14.6. Situation-specific reward
3. Social support		14.7. Reward incompatible behaviour
3.1. Social support (unspecified)	**9. Comparison of outcomes**	14.8. Reward alternative behaviour
3.2. Social support (practical)	9.1. Credible source	
3.3. Social support (emotional)	9.2. Pros and cons	14.9. Reduce reward frequency
	9.3. Comparative imagining of future outcomes	14.10. Remove punishment
4. Shaping knowledge		
4.1. Instruction on how to peform the behaviour	**10. Reward and threat**	**15. Self-belief**
	10.1. Material incentive (behaviour)	15.1. Verbal persuasion about capability
4.2. Information about Antecedents	10.2. Material reward (behaviour)	15.2. Mental rehearsal of successful performance
4.3. Re-attribution	10.3. Non-specific reward	15.3. Focus on past success
4.4. Behavioural experiments	10.4. Social reward	15.4. Self-talk
	10.5. Social incentive	
5. Natural consequences	10.6. Non-specific incentive	**16. Covert learning**
5.1. Information about health consequences	10.7. Self-incentive	16.1. Imaginary punishment
	10.8. Incentive (outcome)	16.2. Imaginary reward
5.2. Salience of consequences	10.9. Self-reward	16.3. Vicarious consequences
5.3. Information about social and environmental consequences	10.10. Reward (outcome)	
	10.11. Future punishment	
5.4. Monitoring of emotional consequences		
	11. Regulation	
5.5. Anticipated regret	11.1. Pharmacological support	
5.6. Information about emotional consequences	11.2. Reduce negative emotions	
	11.3. Conserving mental resources	
	11.4. Paradoxical instructions	

Table 3.2 Example of BCT label, definition and example from BCTTv1

No.	Label	Definition	Examples
1. Goals and planning			
1.1	Goal setting (behaviour)	Set or agree a goal defined in terms of the behaviour to be achieved *Note: only code[d] goal-setting if there is sufficient evidence that goal set as part of intervention; if goal unspecified or a behavioural outcome, code **1.3, Goal setting (outcome)**; if the goal defines a specific context, frequency, duration or intensity for the behaviour, also code **1.4, Action planning***	Agree a daily walking goal (e.g. 3 miles) with the person and reach agreement about the goal Set the goal of eating 5 pieces of fruit per day as specified in public health guidelines

[d] References to coding relate to using the Taxonomy to describe the content of published interventions.

Linking intervention functions with BCTs

The first step is to consider all the BCTs that could be considered for any particular function. BCTs appropriate for each function, as judged by a consensus of four experts in behaviour change, are shown in Table 3.3. When considering BCTs, it is essential to be guided by the definition not by the label (see Appendix 4). The next step is to narrow the 'long list' of BCTs down to ones that are most likely to be appropriate for the situation in which you are intervening. In addition to considering the APEASE criteria (Table 1), another way of narrowing down the list is to first consider BCTs used most frequently[5] before considering less frequently used BCTs. These are also shown in bold in Table 3.3. It should be noted that the BCTs in BCTTv1 have been identified mostly from interventions directly targeting individuals and so are represented more frequently by some intervention functions (especially 'enablement') than others (most notably 'restriction' which does not feature in BCTTv1. Linking the BCW to BCTs has drawn attention to the need to develop taxonomies of BCTs across all the intervention functions. This will require detailed analyses of interventions targeting community, organisational and population levels in much the same way as has been done for interventions directly targeting individuals.

---

[5] BCTs were identified in a study using the BCT Taxonomy v1 to identify intervention content and defined as frequently used if they appeared in 16 or more of 40 intervention descriptions included in the study [72].

150

Table 3.3 Linking intervention functions to BCTs

Intervention function	Individual BCTs
Education	**Most frequently used BCTs:** • Information about social and environmental consequences • Information about health consequences • Feedback on behaviour • Feedback on outcome(s) of the behaviour • Prompts/cues • Self-monitoring of behaviour Less frequently used BCTs: • Biofeedback • Self-monitoring of outcome(s) of behaviour • Cue signalling reward • Satiation • Information about antecedents • Re-attribution • Behavioural experiments • Information about emotional consequences • Information about others' approval
Persuasion	**Most frequently used BCTs:** • Credible source • Information about social and environmental consequences • Information about health consequences • Feedback on behaviour • Feedback on outcome(s) of the behaviour Less frequently used BCTs: • Biofeedback • Re-attribution • Focus on past success • Verbal persuasion about capability • Framing/reframing • Identity associated with changed behaviour • Identification of self as role model • Information about emotional consequences • Salience of consequences • Information about others' approval • Social comparison

Table continued.

Incentivisation	Most frequently used BCTs: • Feedback on behaviour • Feedback on outcome(s) of behaviour • Monitoring of behaviour by others without evidence of feedback • Monitoring outcome of behaviour by others without evidence of feedback • Self-monitoring of behaviour Less frequently used BCTs: • Paradoxical instructions • Biofeedback • Self-monitoring of outcome(s) of behaviour • Cue signalling reward • Remove aversive stimulus • Reward approximation • Rewarding completion • Situation-specify reward • Reward incompatible behaviour • Reduce reward frequency • Reward alternate behaviour • Remove punishment • Social reward • Material reward • Material reward (outcome) • Self-reward • Non-specific reward • Incentive • Behavioural contract • Commitment • Discrepancy between current behaviour and goal • Imaginary reward

Coercion	**Most frequently used BCTs:** • Feedback on behaviour • Feedback on outcome(s) of behaviour • Monitoring of behaviour by others without evidence of feedback • Monitoring outcome of behaviour by others without evidence of feedback • Self-monitoring of behaviour Less frequently used BCTs: • Biofeedback • Self-monitoring of outcome(s) of behaviour • Remove access to the reward • Punishment • Behaviour cost • Remove reward • Future punishment • Behavioural contract • Commitment • Discrepancy between current behaviour and goal • Incompatible beliefs • Anticipated regret • Imaginary punishment
Training	**Most frequently used BCTs:** • Demonstration of the behaviour • Instruction on how to perform a behaviour • Feedback on the behaviour • Feedback on outcome(s) of behaviour • Self-monitoring of behaviour • Behavioural practice/rehearsal Less frequently used BCTs: • Biofeedback • Self-monitoring of outcome(s) of behaviour • Habit formation • Habit reversal • Graded tasks • Behavioural experiments • Mental rehearsal of successful performance • Self-talk • Self-reward

Table continued.

Restriction	No BCTs in BCTTv1 are linked to this intervention function because they are focused on changing the way that people think, feel and react rather than the way the external environment limits their behaviour.
Environmental restructuring	**Most frequently used BCTs:** • **Adding objects to the environment** • **Prompts/cues** • **Restructuring the physical environment** Less frequently used BCTs: • Cue signalling reward • Remove access to the reward • Remove aversive stimulus • Satiation • Exposure • Associative learning • Reduce prompt/cue • Restructuring the social environment
Modelling	**Most frequently used BCTs:** • **Demonstration of the behaviour**
Enablement	**Most frequently used BCTs:** • **Social support (unspecified)** • **Social support (practical)** • **Goal setting (behaviour)** • **Goal setting (outcome)** • **Adding objects to the environment** • **Problem solving** • **Action planning** • **Self-monitoring of behaviour** • **Restructuring the physical environment** • **Review behaviour goal(s)** • **Review outcome goal(s)**

	Less frequently used BCTs: • Social support (emotional) • Reduce negative emotions • Conserve mental resources • Pharmacological support • Self-monitoring of outcome(s) of behaviour • Behaviour substitution • Overcorrection • Generalisation of a target behaviour • Graded tasks • Avoidance/reducing exposure to cues for the behaviour • Restructuring the social environment • Distraction • Body changes • Behavioural experiments • Mental rehearsal of successful performance • Focus on past success • Self-talk • Verbal persuasion about capability • Self-reward • Behavioural contract • Commitment • Discrepancy between current behaviour and goal • Pros and cons • Comparative imagining of future outcomes • Valued self-identity • Framing/reframing • Incompatible beliefs • Identity associated with changed behaviour • Identification of self as role model • Salience of consequences • Monitoring of emotional consequences • Anticipated regret • Imaginary punishment • Imaginary reward • Vicarious consequences

Linking TDF domains with BCTs

Some intervention designers proceed directly from understanding the behaviour using the TDF to selecting BCTs for the intervention (see [44] for an example of this process). This process has been guided by a matrix of domains and BCTs developed using the 2005 version of the TDF and a preliminary list of BCTs [49]. An example of how this process has been applied to design an intervention to promote adherence to evidence based-guidelines is shown in Box 3.3 at the end of this chapter. More recent work drawing on an expert consensus exercise using the 2012 update and BCTs has linked 12 of the domains to 59 BCTs from BCT Taxonomy v1. For those wishing to use this approach, this linking is shown in Table 3.4 [73].

Table 3.4 Expert consensus linking BCTs to TDF domains

TDF domain	BCT
Knowledge	Health consequences Biofeedback Antecedents Feedback on behaviour
Skills	Graded tasks Behavioural rehearsal / practice Habit reversal Body changes Habit formation
Professional Role and Identity	No BCTs are linked to this domain

Beliefs about Capabilities	Verbal persuasion to boost self-efficacy Focus on past Success
Optimism	Verbal persuasion to boost self-efficacy
Beliefs about Consequences	Emotional consequences Salience of consequences Covert sensitisation Anticipated regret Social and environmental consequences Comparative imagining of future outcomes Vicarious reinforcement Threat Pros and cons Covert conditioning
Reinforcement	Threat Self-reward Differential reinforcement Incentive Thinning Negative reinforcement Shaping Counter conditioning Discrimination training Material reward Social reward Non-specific reward Response cost Anticipation of future rewards or removal of punishment Punishment Extinction Classical conditioning
Intentions	Commitment Behavioural contract

Table continued.

Goals	Goal setting (outcome) Goal setting (behaviour) Review of outcome goal(s) Review behaviour goals Action planning (including implementation intentions)
Memory, Attention and Decision Processes	No BCTs are linked to this domain
Environmental Context and Resources	Restructuring the physical environment Discriminative (learned) cue Prompts / cues Restructuring the social environment Avoidance / changing exposure to cues for the behaviour
Social Influences	Social comparison Social support or encouragement (general) Information about others' approval Social support (emotional) Social support (practical) Vicarious reinforcement Restructuring the social environment Modelling or demonstrating the behaviour Identification of self as role model Social reward
Emotion	Reduce negative emotions Emotional consequences Self-assessment of affective consequences Social support (emotional)
Behavioural Regulation	Self-monitoring of behaviour

How to identify BCTs - completing Worksheet 7

Worksheet 7 asks you to identify BCTs based on the intervention functions selected in Step 5; we selected incentivisation and enablement. For our example we will start by identifying the most frequently used BCTs that are relevant to these intervention functions and consider their appropriateness in terms of how well they meet the APEASE criteria in the context of promoting the cleaning hands using alcohol gel (Table 3.5).

Table 3.5 Example of a completed Worksheet 7

Intervention function	COM-B component	Most recently used BCTs	Does the BCT meet the APEASE criteria (affordability, practicability, effectiveness/ cost-effectiveness, acceptability, side-effects/safety, equity) in the context of cleaning hands using alcohol gel?
Incentivisation	Reflective motivation	Feedback on behaviour	Yes
	Automatic motivation	Feedback on outcome(s) of behaviour	Yes
		Monitoring of behaviour by others without evidence of feedback	Yes
		Monitoring outcome of behaviour by others without evidence of feedback	Unlikely to be effective in this context.
		Self-monitoring of behaviour	Not practicable to deliver.

Box continued.

Enablement	Psychological capability	Social support (unspecified)	Unlikely to be effective in this context
	Social opportunity	Social support (practical)	Unlikely to be effective in this context
	Automatic motivation		
		Goal setting (behaviour)	Yes
		Goal setting (outcome)	Yes
		Adding objects to the environment	Not relevant in this context
		Problem solving	Not relevant in this context
		Action planning	Yes
		Self-monitoring of behaviour	Not practicable to deliver
		Restructuring the physical environment	Not relevant in this context
		Review behaviour goal(s)	Yes
		Review outcome goal(s)	Not relevant in this context

Frequently used BCTs selected:
Feedback on behaviour
Feedback on outcome(s) of behaviour
Monitoring of behaviour by others without evidence of feedback
Goal setting (behaviour)
Goal setting (outcome)
Action planning
Review behaviour goal(s)

Drafting an intervention strategy to increase hand hygiene behaviour amongst hospital staff
Below we summarise the intervention functions, policy categories and BCTs that we have systematically selected to address the drivers of our target behaviour identified in the behavioural diagnosis. To this we have added a less frequently used BCT, 'non-specific reward' as this also meets the APEASE criteria in this context. Based on this selection we can now draft an intervention strategy, describing how BCTs will be delivered in this context and through the policy categories selected. The example is based on the Feedback Intervention Trial (FIT) which developed and evaluated an intervention using COM-B and the TDF. It was found, using a stepped wedge design across 16 UK hospitals, to be effective in increasing staff hand-hygiene behaviour [74] (Table 3.6).

Table 3.6 Example of a completed draft intervention strategy

Intervention functions	COM-B components served by intervention functions	Policy categories through which BCTs can be delivered[e]	Intervention strategy BCTs delivered in an extract from the Feedback Intervention Trial (Fuller et al. 2012)
Incentivisation	Reflective motivation Automatic motivation	Service provision	The intervention was delivered by a 'ward co-ordinator' who observed hand hygiene practices of staff individually and in groups. Following observation, staff received feedback individually and in group meetings on the percentage of times the behaviour was appropriately performed. (BCT - feedback on behaviour). In cases of 100% compliance with hand hygiene practice staff received a certificate and feedback at their annual appraisal (BCT – non-specific reward). Where staff members were observed not cleaning their hands, a goal was set to clean their hands in identified high risk situations (BCT – goal setting behaviour) and an action plan formed to support achieving the goal (BCT – action planning).
Enablement	Psychological capability Social opportunity Automatic motivation		

[e] In Step 6, although communication/marketing and service provision were identified as potentially useful policy categories through which to deliver the intervention, the intervention strategy shown here is delivered through service provision only.

This strategy illustrates how the BCTs 'feedback on behaviour', 'non-specific reward', 'goal setting (behaviour)' and 'action planning' could be delivered through changes to service provision in order to enable and incentivise staff to clean their hands using alcohol gel.

Designers are encouraged to pilot, review and amend the strategy as necessary with input from key stakeholders before launching the intervention. Process and outcome data should be collected to allow regular review and further improvement as necessary.

Now it's your turn!
Please complete Worksheet 7

Case study examples of using BCTs in intervention design, to specify intervention content and inform evidence-based policy

An example of using BCTs identified in effective interventions to inform policy is given in Box 3.2.

Box 3.2 Using BCTs to inform evidence-based policy – the example of smoking cessation

The formulation of smoking cessation policy in England is an example of linking BCTs to evidence-based policy. Eight BCTs associated with higher success rates for smoking cessation were identified in published reports of effective interventions in a Cochrane review [75] and in the treatment manuals of English Stop Smoking services where the delivery of these techniques was compared with self-report and CO-verified quit rates [76]. The BCTs are summarized below together with the intervention function they serve (Table 3.7 - note these techniques are from a taxonomy of BCTs identified in behavioural support for smoking cessation [7] so the labels will be different to those in BCTTv1).

Table 3.7: Effective BCTs in smoking cessation linked to intervention functions

BCT	Intervention function
1. Provide information on consequences of smoking and smoking cessation	Education, persuasion
2. Measure CO	Education, persuasion, incentivisation, coercion, training
3. Facilitate barrier identification and problem solving	Enablement

4. Facilitate relapse prevention and coping	Enablement
5. Facilitate goal setting	Enablement
6. Advise on stop-smoking medication	Education
7. Give options for additional and later support	Enablement
8. Provide information on withdrawal symptoms	Education, persuasion

The intervention functions these BCTs are linked to can all be delivered through the policy categories service provision and guidelines. As a result, these BCTs now form the basis of the national, consensually determined set of competences for smoking cessation practitioners adopted by the NHS (policy category - guidelines) for the delivery of behavioural support in English Stop Smoking Services (policy category – service provision). This formed the basis of a national training programme, see www.ncsct.co.uk.

An example of selecting BCTs in intervention design based on formal theories is shown in Box 3.3.

Box 3.3 Selecting BCTs for an intervention using formal theories – the example of physical activity in school children

Development of a theory-based intervention to enhance physical activity among adolescents [77]

Aims: To develop a school-based physical activity (PA) intervention for adolescents in Portugal.

Methods: Using formal theories, Social Cognitive and Self-regulation Theories (SCT and SRT), 21 behaviour change techniques from Abraham and Michie's BCT taxonomy [3] were used to target the following SCT and SRT theoretical determinants of behaviour: general knowledge, outcome expectancies, self-efficacy, and behavioural intentions (from SCT) and action planning and coping planning (from SRT).

BCTs used: Provide general information, provide information on consequences, provide information on others' approval, prompt intention formation, prompt specific goal setting, set graded tasks, prompt barrier identification, agreement of behavioural contract, provide instruction, demonstration of behaviour, prompt behaviour practice, prompt self-monitoring, provide feedback, provide general encouragement, provide contingent rewards, teach to use prompts/cues, use follow up prompts, provide opportunities for social comparison, plan social support, prompt identification as role model, relapse prevention. Example items include: 'If I continue with my current level of PA....', 'I intend to engage in PA three times a week', and 'I am certain that I can engage in PA three times per week'. SRT constructs were measured pre and post intervention using items such as: 'I have made a detailed plan regarding when and how to engage in PA' and 'I have made a detailed plan regarding what to do if something interferes with my plans (e.g. If I have a test that week').

Self-reported PA was measured at baseline, directly after the intervention, three and nine months. SCT constructs were measured pre and post intervention.

Two examples of selecting BCTs in intervention design based on the TDF is shown in Box 3.4

Box 3.4 Selecting BCTs for an intervention using the TDF – the example of adherence to evidence-based guidelines

Evidence-based care of older people with suspected cognitive impairment in general practice: the IRIS cluster randomised trial [78]

Aims: To design and test an intervention to promote Australian GPs' adherence to two recommendations in clinical guidelines for dementia: i) receipt of a formal cognitive assessment; ii) assessment of depression using a validated scale.

Methods: Interviews based on the TDF were conducted with GPs to identify barriers and facilitators to adhering to the two recommendations. Relevant domains were linked to BCTs using the matrix resulting from the expert consensus process[49].

Results: The trial protocol reported barriers and facilitators for one recommendation - receipt of a formal cognitive assessment (the barriers and facilitators for assessing co-morbid depression using a validated scale are available in Murphy et al [79]):

Barriers: Beliefs about consequences' (GPs held negative beliefs about formal cognitive testing); 'emotion' (GPS were not comfortable carrying out the assessments; 'skills' (GPs had limited training to carry out assessments); 'beliefs about capabilities' (GPs had limited confidence carrying out assessments); 'environmental context and resources' (GPs had limited access to tests or did not have the time or resources to carryout out the tests); 'social influences' (patients found the tests uncomfortable or they or their family refused testing.

Facilitators: 'Knowledge' (knowing when an assessment is needed); 'skills' (knowing how to carry out an assessment); 'beliefs about capabilities' (being confident to carry out assessments); 'environmental context and resources' (having enough time and resources to carry out assessments).

The following BCTs identified by the matrix were delivered in a workshop with GPs: *information provision, persuasive communication; information regarding behaviour, outcome; feedback; social processes of encouragement, pressure, support; self-monitoring; modelling/ demonstration of behaviour by others; increasing skills; coping skills; rehearsal of relevant skills; and action planning* (note the labels of the BCTs were from an earlier taxonomy and so may be slightly different than those in BCTTv1).

Conclusion: This is an example of using a theory-based tool to understand behaviour and then systematically selecting BCTs to change the target behaviour and test the resulting intervention in a randomised controlled trial.

Development of a behaviour change intervention: a case study on the practical application of theory [80]

Aim: To develop a behaviour change intervention to enhance GPs' adherence to clinical guidelines for consultations with patients with osteoarthritis.

Method: Intervention development followed the 'Implementation of Change Model' [81], which provides evidence-based and step-by-step guidance to implementing change in clinical practice. Guidance on what constitutes a 'model' osteoarthritis consultation was developed through a consensus exercise, and meetings

Box continued.

were held with three advisory groups (two consisting of GPs in teaching or research roles; one consisting of primary healthcare practitioners from a general practice). The groups were asked about:

1. Their current clinical management of osteoarthritis.
2. Their awareness of, and agreement with, NICE guidelines on osteoarthritis.
3. Perceived discrepancies between their own practice and NICE guidance/model consultation.
4. Opinions about barriers to and incentives for delivering the model consultation.

Responses to these questions were coded into the domains of the TDF.

Results: The TDF domains identified were used to guide the selection of BCTs for the intervention, informed by expert consensus as to which techniques are most likely to effect change for each of the domains [49]. Identified domains and chosen techniques are shown in Table 3.8.

Table 3.8 TDF domains linked to BCTs delivered in the intervention

TDF Domain	Behaviour Change Technique
Knowledge	Information provision
Skills	Rehearsal of relevant skills; graded task starting with easy tasks; increasing skills: problem-solving
Social/professional role and identity	Social processes of encouragement, pressure and support
Beliefs about capabilities	Social processes of encouragement, pressure and support
Beliefs about consequences	Information provision; persuasive communication
Motivation and goals	Contract; rewards; persuasive communication
Memory, attention and decision processes	Prompts, triggers, cues

Using the TDF alongside a practical model for changing clinical behaviour meant that a systematically developed theory-based complex intervention could be developed in a step-by-step and very 'do-able' manner.

An example of using BCTTv1 to describe the content of an intervention and specify its mechanism of action, by linking to the COM-B model and TDF, is given in Box 3.5.

Box 3.5 Describing intervention content and mechanism of action using BCTTv1, BCW and TDF

Describing an intervention to support implementation: improving compliance with the 'Sepsis Six' care pathway [19].

Background: Sepsis is a systemic, deleterious response to infection leading to acute organ dysfunction and has a mortality rate of 40%. Severe sepsis is estimated to kill 37,000 in UK hospitals annually and consume 50% of critical care resources. Mortality can be halved if treated within the hour by implementing the 'Sepsis Six' care pathway: high flow oxygen, blood cultures, intravenous fluid & antibiotics, haemoglobin & lactate levels, measuring urine output.

A pragmatic nurse-led intervention to increase compliance with the Sepsis Six pathway was piloted in several wards of a large NHS hospital in London. Once 95% compliance was reached in pilot wards, the aim was to implement the Sepsis Six pathway in all wards. A first step in optimising implementation is to understand the content of the intervention by describing its active ingredients and drivers of behaviour it intends to target.

Aim: To use the BCW, BCTTv1 and the TDF to describe the intervention's content and mechanisms of action in order to facilitate implementation across settings.

Method: A detailed description of the intervention was obtained through analysis of (i) intervention documents, (ii) interviews with nurses and the intervention facilitator and (iii) observations of training and feedback sessions on pilot wards. A written description of the intervention was checked for accuracy by the implementation team. The BCW and BCTTv1 were used to code the functions of the intervention and its BCTs. The drivers of behaviour that each BCT was intended to target were mapped to the domains of the TDF and the COM-B model to identify their mechanisms of action.

Results: The description revealed six intervention functions (see Table 3.9).

- 'Education' to improve knowledge of susceptibility and severity of Sepsis and effectiveness of pathway.
- 'Training' to impart skills for pathway implementation
- 'Persuasion' to change beliefs and encourage action towards implementation
- 'Enablement' to increase means and reduce barriers for compliance
- 'Environmental restructuring' to improve physical opportunity to implement
- 'Incentivisation' to create an expectation of reward for pathway compliance

Table 3.9 Content and mechanisms of change of the first eight BCTs (see Appendix 5 for the full version and below for key to abbreviations)

| | | CAPABILITY | | | OPPORTUNITY | | MOTIVATION | | | | | |
| | | Physical | Psychological | | Social | Physical | Reflective | | | | | Auto |
BCT	Functions	Text description	Skills	Knowledge	Memory, attention & decision processes	Behavioural regulation	Social influences	Environmental context and resources	Beliefs about capabilities	Beliefs about consequences	Social professional role & identity	Optimism	Goals	Emotions
Information about health consequences	Education, Persuasion	Staff were told about dangers of Sepsis and effectiveness of following pathway.		▓						▓				
Salience of consequences	Persuasion	Staff were told a story of a young patient who had died from Sepsis needlessly.												▓
Social comparison	Persuasion	Staff were told about high compliance on other wards.					▓				▓			
Demonstration of behaviour	Training	Staff observed & participated in Sepsis Six training simulations.	▓		▓	▓								
Instruction on how to perform the behaviour	Education		▓		▓	▓								
Behavioural practice/ rehearsal Habit formation	Training		▓		▓	▓								
Feedback on behaviour	Persuasion	Staff compliance was monitored by board and intervention implementers and verbal feedback was given in group meetings.				▓					▓			

174

This exercise showed the intervention to be more complex than the developers had realised. Specifying it using theory and BCT methodology provided a more comprehensive understanding of its components, aims and functions.

Step 8: Identify mode of delivery

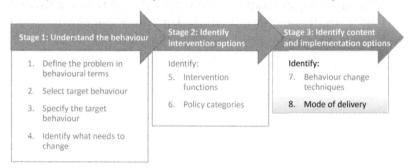

As well as identifying BCTs (Worksheet 7), decisions need to be made about the mode or modes of delivery for the intervention. Mode of delivery is one of seven dimensions of interventions identified [82]. The others are content (what was delivered); provider (who delivered it); setting (where it was delivered); recipient (to whom it was delivered); intensity (over how many contacts it was delivered); duration (over what period of time it was delivered); fidelity (the extent to which it was delivered as intended). In reports of interventions, there is often insufficient distinction made between intervention content and mode of delivery (e.g. telephone, face-to face) and often more detail about mode of delivery than content (i.e. the putative active ingredients).

Just as for intervention content and implementation through policy levers, it is important to consider the full panoply of possible modes of delivering interventions before deciding the most appropriate for the particular target behaviour, population group and setting. A simple taxonomy of modes of delivery is given in Figure 3.1.

Clearly this only applies to a limited subset of intervention functions, but it should provide a start in thinking about how interventions can be delivered.

Figure 3.1 Taxonomy of modes of delivery for intervention functions that involve communication

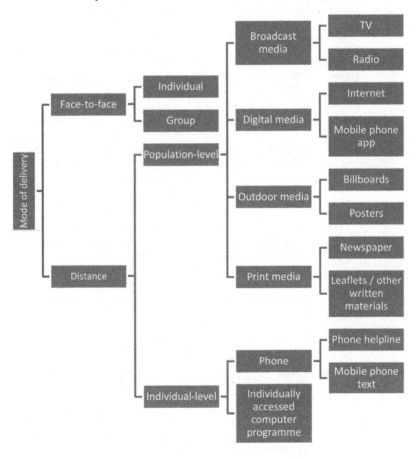

Table 3.10 illustrates different modes of delivery used to deliver interventions with one target: smoking cessation

Table 3.10 Examples of different modes of delivery used to deliver smoking cessation interventions

Mode of delivery				Example
Face-to-face	Individual			One-to-one behavioural support for smoking cessation in English NHS Stop Smoking Services [70]
	Group			Group behavioural support programmes for smoking cessation [83]
Distance	Population-level	Broadcast media	TV	A TV advert describing the toxic damage tobacco smoke does to vital organs - part of the Smokefree campaign, NHS, UK. http://www.youtube.com/user/smokefreevideos
			Radio	A radio advert aired in Victoria, Australia describing the symptoms of emphysema [84]
		Outdoor media	Billboard	A billboard advertising showing clotted blood dripping from a cigarette - part of the Smokefree campaign, NHS, UK. http://www.nhs.uk/smokefree
			Poster	Posters encouraging referral to a Liverpool hospital stop smoking service displayed as part of the "Time to Quit" campaign [85]
		Print media	Newspaper	Newspaper adverts delivering anti-tobacco messages [86]
			Leaflet	A leaflet highlighting the link between smoking and cervical cancer [87]
		Digital media	Internet	StopAdvisor – a theory-based interactive internet-based smoking cessation intervention [88]
			Mobile phone app	Smoke Free 28 (SF28) – A theory-based smoking cessation app [89]
	Individual-level	Phone	Phone helpline	Behavioural support for smoking cessation delivered over the phone. [90]
			Mobile phone text	txt2stop – a smoking cessation programme delivered via mobile phone text messaging [91]
		Individually accessed computer programme		Quitkey - A hand-held computer that creates a tailored smoking cessation program [92]

In selecting the preferred mode or modes of delivery, the APEASE criteria (Table 1, p23) should be considered:

- **Affordability:** Cost considerations when selecting mode of delivery include not only how much it will cost to design but also how much it will cost to deliver. There are extensive costs when designing a website or mobile phone app but these are then relatively cheap to deliver once launched or made available for download. In comparison, a face-to-face intervention is likely to be less expensive to design than to deliver.

- **Practicability:** The selected mode of delivery should allow for the intervention to be delivered as designed. Some BCTs might be more effectively delivered through certain modes of delivery. For example, action planning or self-monitoring of the behaviour are more likely to be effective when delivered face to-face or over the phone rather than by billboard or poster.

- **Effectiveness and cost-effectiveness:** Where it exists, evidence of (cost-) effectiveness should be key in guiding selection of mode of delivery. Where the evidence base is lacking, other APEASE criteria should be used to guide selection.

- **Acceptability:** As illustrated in Table 1 in the Introduction (p23), how acceptable a mode of delivery is should be considered in terms of the recipient, those delivering the intervention and whether it is aligned with political objectives.

- **Side-effects/safety**: Intervention designers should explore potential unintended consequences of modes of delivery under consideration. For example, an intervention targeting an identified and potentially life-threatening gap in health professional practice might result in unnecessary panic if delivered via broadcast or print media than face-to-face.

- **Equity:** Asking whether selecting a particular mode of delivery will result in the intervention reaching the intended recipients or whether it will disadvantage some groups will guide considerations around equity. For example when using digital media technologies, consider whether all intended groups of intervention recipients have broadly equal access.

An additional consideration when identifying mode of delivery relates to evaluating the intervention. Delivering an intervention face-to-face will allow the designer potentially to obtain more information about intervention recipients and to follow them up when evaluating the effect of the intervention. However, whilst broadcast media has the potential to reach more people than other modes of delivery, intervention recipients are not as easy to identify when evaluating the effectiveness of an intervention.

How to identify mode of delivery – completing Worksheet 8

In this worksheet you are asked to identify the modes(s) through which the intervention will be delivered. In selecting relevant BCTs in the previous step we have already started to hint at the modes we might use to deliver these BCTs such as direct observation and face-to-face feedback on hand hygiene behaviour.

An example of using a systematic approach to selecting a mode of delivery is delivering the BCT, 'feedback on the behaviour' to hospital staff to increase the frequency of cleaning their hands using alcohol gel. This could be delivered face-to-face in meetings at the individual or group level, by written report on the proportion of staff members observed cleaning their hands or by an SMS messaging service or smartphone application. Where there is no effectiveness evidence to inform the choice, the APEASE criteria are a useful guide. Below we show the application of the APEASE criteria in relation to increasing hand hygiene in the UK hospital context (Table 3.11).

Table 3.11 Example of a completed Worksheet 8

Mode of delivery				Does the mode of delivery meet the APEASE criteria (affordability, practicability, effectiveness/cost-effectiveness, acceptability, side-effects/safety, equity) in the context of cleaning hands using alcohol gel?
Face-to-face	Individual			Yes
	Group			Yes
Dis-tance	Popula-tion-level	Broadcast media	TV	These modes of delivery are not relevant as ward staff are unlikely to have access to phones, computers or be exposed to other forms of media whilst working on hospital wards.
			Radio	
		Outdoor media	Billboard	
			Poster	
		Print media	Newspaper	
			Leaflet	
		Digital media	Internet	
			Mobile phone app	
	Individu-al-level	Phone	Phone helpline	
			Mobile phone text	
		Individually accessed computer programme		

Now it's your turn!
Please complete Worksheet 8

Chapter 4: A case study using the BCW to design an intervention to prevent melioidosis in Northeast Thailand

With permission from Assistant Professor Direk Limmathurotsakul (Head of Microbiology Department, Mahidol-Oxford Tropical Medicine Research Unit; Wellcome Trust (101103/Z/13/Z))

This chapter is a case study of applying all eight steps from the BCW method described in Chapters 1-3 to design an intervention to address a real world problem that is currently causing thousands of deaths a year.

Aim

Melioidosis is an infectious disease caused by exposure to a Gram-negative bacterium, Burkholderia pseudomallei. Diabetes is a major risk factor for melioidosis resulting in 40% mortality. Northern Thailand, the context for this intervention, has a very high incidence of melioidosis.

The intervention described in this case study is being designed and trialled as part of a strategy to persuade Thai authorities to implement policies to reduce incidence of melioidosis. This piece of work will generate evidence to inform which policies might be most appropriate in bringing about change.

This case study has resulted as a piece of consultancy work between the BCW team and the melioidosis study team based at Mahidol-Oxford Tropical Medicine Research Unit in Thailand.

Methods

This case study applies the theory-based, systematic eight-step method using the BCW, TDF, BCTs described in Chapters 1-3 to design an intervention to prevent melioidosis.

Results

Here we set out how each of the eight steps has informed the next in the intervention design process:

Step 1: Define the problem in behavioural terms
The first step is to define who is involved in the behaviour and what the behaviour is. In this context the target individual, group or population involved in the behaviour are adults with diabetes and the behaviour is having contact with the bacteria that causes melioidosis.

Step 2: Select the target behaviour
Having defined the behavioural problem, the next step is to list all of the behaviours that could potentially prevent development of melioidosis. Based on previous work, the melioidosis study team recommended the following preventative behaviours:

1. Avoid direct contact with soil or environmental water

2. If contact is necessary, wear protective gear

3. In the event of an injury involving contamination, immediately clean with soap and clean water

4. Keep open wounds covered and avoid contact with soil or water until completely healed

5. Always wear shoes, do not walk bare foot

6. Only drink bottled or boiled water

7. Do not eat food contaminated with soil or dust

8. When outside avoid rain or dust clouds

9. Do not smoke

10. Be aware that you are at greater risk of melioidosis if you have certain conditions, including diabetes, chronic kidney disease, and diseases that require steroid therapy or medications that suppress the immune system.

11. Please visit the community hospital if you feel sick, have a high fever and do not feel better after self-supportive treatment such as paracetamol, drink a lot of water, resting and sleeping within 24 to 48 hours.

In collaboration with the BCW team, refinements were made in order to produce a behaviourally specific and coherently grouped list of potential behaviours:

Items 1) 'avoid direct contact with soil or environmental water' and 8) 'when outside avoid rain or dust clouds' were separated out into individual behaviours, e.g. 'avoid direct contact with soil' (one behaviour), 'avoid direct contact with environmental water' (another behaviour). This is because the drivers of these two behaviours (and therefore what might be needed to change them) might be quite different. The exception here is item 2) 'if contact with soil or environmental water is necessary, wear protective gear'. Although we considered this to be two behaviours (i) wear protective gear if in contact with soil; (ii) wear protective gear if in contact with environmental water; it was retained as one behaviour because the two situations coincide so frequently.

Item 10 was removed from the list as being aware of being at greater risk of melioidosis is not a behaviour but a cognitive antecedent to behaviour.

We noted in the refined list of behaviours that some behaviours should always be performed whereas others are to be performed only under certain conditions. Some behaviours are about doing something and others about not doing something. On this basis we grouped the behaviours in terms of whether they are protective (do) or avoidant (don't do) and whether they are to be performed always or conditionally (only under certain conditions) see Table 4.1.

Table 4.1 Potential behaviours to prevent melioidosis

	Always	Conditional
Avoid (don't do)	Avoid direct contact with soil Avoid direct contact with environmental water Do not eat food contaminated with soil or dust Do not smoke	When having open wounds, avoid contact between open wounds and soil or water When outside, avoid rain When outside, avoid dust clouds
Protective (do)	Always wear shoes (do not walk bare foot) Drink bottled water Boil water before drinking	If contact with soil or environmental water is necessary, wear protective gear In the event of an injury involving contamination, immediately clean with soap and clean water Keep open wounds covered Please visit community hospital if you feel sick, have a high fever and do not feel better after self-supportive treatment (such as paracetamol, drink a lot of water, resting and sleeping) within 24 to 48 hours

Following the 'less is more' principle of intervention design, a small set of target behaviours was selected for intensive intervention rather than a less focussed, 'scattergun' approach to attempting to change more behaviours.

To select the behaviours we considered the: (i) likely impact of changing each of the behaviours on preventing melioidosis; (ii) ease with which behaviours could be changed; (iii) generalisation of 'spillover' effects in terms of the impact on related behaviours; (iv) extent to which the behaviour can be easily measured. On this basis, the target behaviours selected were: boiling water before drinking and wearing protective gear when coming into contact with soil or environmental water were selected as target behaviours.

Step 3: Specify the target behaviour
The selected target behaviours are described in as much detail as possible according to who, what, where, when, how often and with whom they were to be performed (see Table 4.2). Note here how 'protective gear' has been defined as long rubber boots.

Table 4.2 Behavioural specification of target behaviours

	Target behaviour	
Specification criteria	Boil water before drinking	Wear protective gear when coming into contact with soil or environmental water
Who needs to perform the behaviour?	Anyone in the house capable of using a kettle or stove	Adults with diabetes coming into contact with soil or environmental water
What do they need to do differently to achieve the desired change?	Boil water before drinking it	Put on long rubber boots
When do they need to do it?	Long enough in advance to ensure a supply of cold drinking water	Before coming into contact with soil or environmental water
Where do they need to do it?	At home	Anywhere there is likely to be contact with soil or environmental water
How often do they need to do it?	Every day to ensure a supply of cold drinking water	Every time they come into contact with soil or environmental water
With whom do they need to do it?	Not dependent on others	Not dependent on others

Step 4: Identify what needs to change
Having selected and specified the target behaviours, a behavioural analysis using the COM-B model is used to determine what needs to happen for each target behaviour to occur and what, in terms of capability, motivation and/ or opportunity, needs to shift in the current context. The behavioural analyses and resulting behavioural diagnoses for both selected target behaviours are shown in Tables 4.3-4.4.

Table 4.3 Behavioural analysis of target behaviour: Boil water before drinking

COM-B Components	What needs to happen for the target behaviour to occur?	Is there a need for change?
Physical capability	Be able to boil water before drinking	No change needed
Psychological capability	Know to boil water before drinking Know how to establish reminders, routines and habits to boil water before drinking Advanced planning skills to ensure a supply of cooled boiled water	Change needed
Physical opportunity	Have a water container and stove	No change needed
Social opportunity	Acceptability and expectations of boiling water before drinking	Change needed
Reflective motivation	Intend to and prioritise boiling water before drinking	Change needed
Automatic motivation	Establish reminders, routines and habits to boil water	Change needed

Behavioural diagnosis:
Psychological capability, social opportunity, reflective and automatic motivation need to change in order for the target behaviour 'boil water before drinking' to occur.

Table 4.4 Behavioural analysis of target behaviour: wear protective gear when coming into contact with soil and environmental water

COM-B Components	What needs to happen for the target behaviour to occur?	Is there a need for change?
Capability: physical	Be able to put on protective gear easily and quickly	Change needed
Capability: psychological	Know that protective gear should be worn when in contact with soil or environmental water. Know how to establish reminders, routines and habits to wear protective gear	Change needed
Opportunity: physical	Have protective gear available	Change needed
Opportunity: social	Acceptability and expectations of wearing protective gear	Change needed
Motivation: reflective	Hold the belief that if they wear protective gear, they will reduce the chance of contracting melioidosis. Intend to and prioritise wearing protective gear	Change needed
Motivation: automatic	Establish routines and habits to wear protective gear	Change needed

Behavioural diagnosis:
Physical and psychological capability, physical and social opportunity, and reflective and automatic motivation need to change in order for the target behaviour 'wearing protective gear when coming into contact with soil or environmental water' to occur.

Step 5: Identify intervention functions
Having identified the drivers of both target behaviours, the next step is to identify the relevant functions that the intervention should serve. Given the overlap in the behavioural diagnoses of the two target behaviours, they were considered together when selecting intervention functions.

According to the linking between COM-B components and intervention functions (see Table 2.3, p116), all intervention functions could potentially bring about the desired change. Table 4.5 shows selection of intervention functions according to practical criteria of relevance, affordability, acceptability, practicability, and likely impact.

Table 4.5 Applying practical criteria to guide intervention function selection

Candidate intervention functions	Is the candidate intervention function relevant, affordable, acceptable, practicable, likely to have impact in this context?
Education	Yes
Persuasion	Yes
Incentivisation	Not practicable or affordable
Coercion	Unlikely to be acceptable
Training	Yes
Restriction	Not practicable or relevant
Environmental restructuring	Yes
Modelling	Yes
Enablement	Yes

Having applied these criteria we have arrived at 6 intervention functions: education, persuasion, training, environmental restructuring, modelling and enablement.

It is worth noting that this was originally conceived of as an educational intervention. By taking the steps described, we can see that in addition to education, there are many other types of intervention that can be used to bring about the desired change. For example, people will need to be persuaded that boiling water before drinking or wearing protective gear will reduce the chances of developing melioidosis and dying from this fatal disease; they will need training in putting on the long rubber boots that can be cumbersome and tricky to get on; the environment will need to be restructured, for example, the addition of the long rubber boots; modelling putting on the boots by patients who have survived melioidosis and the addition of reminder posters will enable people to establish routines and habits of wearing protective gear and boiling water before drinking.

Step 6: Identify policy categories
An important point to note in relation to selecting policy categories through which to deliver interventions is that in this case, the only policy lever available to the designers was service provision. According to Table 2.9 (p138) this policy category can deliver intervention functions: education, persuasion, training, modelling and enablement.

The intervention should be evaluated in a number of small pilot studies, and then the final one will be evaluated in a trial. If found to be effective in preventing melioidosis, designers could potentially access other policy levers, for example, legislation making it compulsory for businesses to provide kettles or urns to boil water and/or fitted long rubber boots for rice farmers exposed to soil or environmental water.

Step 7: Identify behaviour change techniques (BCTs)
Having identified which functions the intervention should serve and through which policy categories the intervention might be delivered, the next step is to identify the intervention content - the BCTs that will bring about change (the 'active ingredients' within the intervention).

The melioidosis study team identified 10 BCTs, but did not use a systematic method for identifying them. We can see that these 10 BCTs covered four of the six relevant intervention functions, but did not include any relating to environmental restructuring or modelling. Table 4.6 shows the 10 BCTs linked to intervention functions, compared to 16 frequently used BCTs [72] deliver all five relevant intervention functions.

Comparing these two ways of identifying BCTs highlights that although BCTs identified by the research team were evidence-based, they do not serve all intervention functions that are likely to be effective in bringing about change. Linking just 16 frequently used BCTs to the same intervention functions demonstrates firstly how all intervention functions are served and secondly that there are more BCTs serving each intervention to select from.

From this long list of BCTs, the next step is to select the ones that are relevant to the local context to make up the final intervention. The following criteria can be applied to this selection: evidence for the effectiveness of the BCT in this context, relevance to the context and the practical criteria of practicability, feasibility and affordability can help to guide selection. It should be noted that the less frequent BCTs identified by the research team, e.g. behavioural experiments, identification of self as a role model and comparative imagining of future outcomes may be selected on the basis of these criteria.

Table 4.6 A comparison of BCTs to bring about change in target behaviours

	BCTs identified by melioidosis prevention research team	Frequently used BCTs
Education	• Behavioural experiments (including hands-on experience of using protective gear) • Self-monitoring of behaviours (daily activity at risks of exposure to the bacteria) • Self-monitoring of outcome behaviours (hospitalisation and infectious diseases) • Information about health consequences (Threat - including education of melioidosis and its potential fatal outcomes)	• Information about social and environmental consequences • Information about health consequences • Feedback on behaviour • Feedback on outcome(s) of behaviour • Prompts/cues • Self-monitoring of behaviour
Persuasion	• Identification of self as a role model • Information about health consequences (Threat - including education of melioidosis and its potential fatal outcomes)	• Credible source • Information about social and environmental consequences • Information about health consequences • Feedback on behaviour • Feedback on outcome(s) of behaviour

Table continued.

Training		
	• Instruction on how to perform the behaviours • Behavioural experiments (including hands-on experience of using protective gear) • Self-monitoring of behaviours (daily activity at risks of exposure to the bacteria) • Self-monitoring of outcome behaviours (hospitalisation and infectious diseases)	• Instruction on how to perform behaviour • Feedback on behaviour • Feedback on outcome(s) of behaviour • Self-monitoring of behaviour • Behavioural practice/ rehearsal
Modelling		• Demonstration of the behaviour
Enablement	• Goal setting • Discrepancy between current behaviours and goal standard • Behavioural experiments (including hands-on experience of using protective gear) • Identification of self as a role model • Review outcome goal • Comparative imagining of future outcomes • Self-monitoring of behaviours (daily activity at risks of exposure to the bacteria) • Self-monitoring of outcome behaviours (hospitalisation and infectious diseases)	• Social support (unspecified) • Social support (practical) • Goal setting (behaviour) • Goal setting (outcome) • Adding objects to the environment • Problem solving • Action planning • Self-monitoring of behaviour • Restructuring the physical environment • Review behaviour goal(s) • Review outcome goal(s)

Step 8: Identify mode of delivery
The original concept for delivery of this intervention was face to face in group sessions at diabetes clinics. If we now consider the kinds of BCTs that could be delivered to bring about change, for example adding objects to the environment (such as the provision of long rubber boots or posters to remind people to boil water or wear long rubber boots) it may be that more than one mode of delivery would be appropriate.

It is often the case that designers will start the design process already constrained to a particular mode(s) of delivery. But as the example above demonstrates, where possible, designers should select the mode of intervention delivery only after selecting the BCTs that will comprise the intervention to ensure that BCTs can be feasibly delivered.

Summary

Using a real world example to work through each of the eight steps of the BCW method highlights the advantages of an explicit, systematic process with each step informing the next.

It also shows the need to apply judgement in selecting intervention functions, BCTs, mode of delivery and, although not relevant here, policy categories. Whilst criteria based on evidence and practical considerations are suggested, designers will need to make judgements on what to select according to their local context.

Chapter 5: A brief guide to using the BCW to evaluate behaviour change interventions and synthesise evidence

Planning the evaluation

Plan how the intervention will be evaluated before and during the design process not after.

Evaluation is key to finding out whether the intervention you have designed has had the outcomes you hoped for. For effective interventions, evaluation can also help to find out how the effect was achieved, that is, the mechanisms of action. This is important for improving interventions. The Medical Research Council's guidance on developing and evaluating complex interventions [11] describe four key stages: development, feasibility and piloting, evaluation and implementation. These form a cycle (Figure 5.1). Thus, evaluation and implementation should be considered before or concurrently with, rather than after, the intervention has been designed. This allows, for example, for outcome and process measures to be matched to BCTs and hypothesised mechanisms of action and for implementation issues to be considered when designing the intervention.

Figure 5.1 Summary of MRC guidance on complex intervention development and evaluation [11]

Feasibility and piloting
Testing procedures
Estimating recruitment & retention
Determining sample size

Development
Identifying the evidence base
Identifying or developing theory
Modelling process and outcomes

Evaluation
Assessing effectiveness
Understanding change process
Assessing cost effectiveness

Implementation
Dissemination
Surveillance and monitoring
Long term follow-up

In this chapter we show how the COM-B model, TDF, BCW and BCTTv1 used in designing interventions (Chapters 1-3) can be used to inform the evaluation of behaviour change interventions in primary studies and in evidence syntheses. They can be used to:

1. identify intervention content (describe content of interventions found to be effective; investigate effectiveness of BCTs in interventions to be evaluated or in evidence synthesis);
2. investigate the functions played by the BCTs;
3. specify theoretical underpinnings and understand processes of change;
4. assess the fidelity of intervention delivery, that is, the extent to which the intervention was delivered as planned; and
5. evaluate other behaviour change frameworks.

We now discuss each of these applications and provide some examples.

1. Identify intervention content

BCTs provide a common language to describe intervention content and characterise interventions. Box 5.1 gives guidance as to how a taxonomy of BCTs used in smoking cessation interventions can be used to identify intervention content. By using BCTs to code intervention content we can investigate the relationship between specific BCTs and intervention effectiveness and identify which BCTs are effective at changing behaviour. For example, this approach has been used to identify self-monitoring as an effective BCT within complex interventions to increase physical activity and healthy eating [93] and to help people reduce excessive alcohol consumption [9]. In these examples, a statistical technique called meta-regression was used; however, it should be noted that this is only possible if there are enough instances of the BCT to give sufficient statistical power for the analysis.

Box 5.1 Coding intervention content

Intervention content can be reported in many ways: a manual or study protocol, peer-review report, transcript of an audio-recorded intervention. If you only have the published report, it is a good idea to contact the authors to ask for the intervention protocol or manual as this will have more detail. A study found that intervention protocols and manuals reported twice as many BCTs as those mentioned in the published reports of the same interventions [94].

Here's an example description of part of an intervention:

'practice nurses attended a ninety-minute practical workshop on chronic obstructive pulmonary disorder including using a spirometer to measure forced vital capacity and how to refer patients to secondary care'

Using BCTTv1 this description would be coded as BCT 4.1 Instruction on how to perform the behaviour as it includes advice on how to perform the behaviour. If we were to code this description using the BCW intervention functions we would code it as 'training' as it involves imparting skills to change behaviour. Invariably this process requires some judgement and workshops on using the BCT Taxonomy (v1): [2] are offered: http://www.ucl.ac.uk/health-psychology/BCTtaxonomy/dissemination.php Instructions on coding intervention content can be found in [95] and are summarised below:

1. Read the transcript first

Having familiarised yourself with the labels and definitions of the taxonomy, read through the intervention description or transcript to get a 'gist' of the topics covered. This might alert you to some BCTs to keep a look out for when you begin to code.

2. Prepare to code

Create a coding framework (this is a list of BCTs and their definitions in the taxonomy with fields to record whether a BCT was used, the location (line and page number) of the intervention description or transcript at which the BCT was identified. This should be repeated each time a BCT is identified.

3. Read the intervention description or transcript in detail and assign a BCT code

Re-read the intervention description or transcript in detail (i.e. line-by-line, sentence-by-sentence). As you read through, highlight the text where a BCT appears to be delivered. Assign the relevant BCT label from the taxonomy to the relevant words of the text. Re-read the taxonomy and check the BCT definitions. Select the BCT with a description that most accurately represents and describes the text under consideration. Highlight the relevant bit of text in the intervention description or transcript and write the appropriate BCT code in the margin next to it (e.g. BM2); do not write out the entire BCT label (e.g. Boost motivation and self-efficacy) as this is space and time consuming. At times, more than one BCT may be assigned to the same section of text.

4. Record relevant information in the coding framework

Record the presence, location and frequency of BCTs in the coding framework as shown in Table 5.1:

Box continued.

Table 5.1 BCT coding framework

BCT CODE	BCT LABEL	BCT DESCRIPTION	SCORE 0= Not Used 1= Used	LINE / PAGE NUMBERS (transcript)	FREQUENCY	TOTAL FREQUENCY
BM1	Provide information on the health consequences of smoking and smoking cessation	Give, or make more salient, information about the physical/health harms caused by smoking and the benefits of stopping; distinguish between the harms from smoking and nicotine; debunk myths about low tar and own-roll cigarettes.	1	05/1 54/2 90/3 120/3	IIII	4

Consider the following when coding descriptions of interventions:

Be clear about the target behaviour – ensure that the BCTs relate to the target behaviour.

Only code what is there - avoid inferences or assumptions that a BCT is present unless there is evidence that it has actually been delivered.

Check BCT definitions - make use of the definitions in the taxonomy you are using to ensure that the BCT label under consideration accurately summarises the text you are trying to code.

Making distinctions - taxonomy-based coding method requires you to make fine distinctions between different behaviours and different BCT labels. Definitions of BCTs vary in the size and scope of activities they cover.. Aim to code at the most specific level.

Multiple BCTS delivered at the same time - you may assign more than one BCT to a single segment of a text as long as there is clear demonstration of both.

BCTs can be used to describe the content of interventions: for those found to be effective, those to be evaluated and those within evidence syntheses.

Describe the content of interventions found to be effective
Ideally BCT taxonomies are used in the intervention design process described in Step 7 of Chapter 3 (pp145-175) but they can be applied post-hoc to evaluated interventions to characterise content. An example of this is the 'Txt2Stop' smoking cessation SMS messaging programme found to double quit rates at 6 months [91]. The 186 core behaviour change messages and 713 additional personalised messages comprising the Txt2Stop intervention were coded using a taxonomy of BCTs developed to code the content of behavioural support sessions for smoking cessation[7].

1,703 BCTs were identified in the 899 text messages. Of these, 870 were to enhance self-regulatory capacity or skills, 552 were to keep users engaged with the intervention, 218 were to maintain motivation to remain abstinent, 39 promoted the use of adjuvant behaviours such as using other NRT medications and 24 were general communication techniques. The coding exercise identified that 90% of instances of BCTs involved only seven BCTs – three were motivational, three self-regulatory and one related to intervention delivery [96]. Coding interventions in this way permits the design of more effective interventions through experimental manipulation of intervention content to establish which components are the active ingredients in the intervention.

Examples of other interventions that have coded content according to BCTs include internet interventions [88], face to face behavioural support for quitting smoking [97], reducing alcohol consumption [9]; and increasing physical activity and healthy eating [37] and condom use [8]. For further examples, see http://www.ucl.ac.uk/health-psychology/BCTtaxonomy/.

Investigate the effectiveness of BCTs in interventions to be evaluated
BCT taxonomies can also be used to identify intervention content and compare this with outcomes in large data sets of routinely collected data. One example is the use of the taxonomy of BCTs used in behavioural support for smoking to identify BCTs present in 43 treatment manuals from a national sample of English Stop Smoking Services [70]. The association between BCTs identified in the manuals and abstinence rates at four weeks were investigated. Nine BCTs were found to be significantly associated with both CO-verified and self-reported 4-week abstinence rates. These nine BCTs targeted the following functions:

- Capability - *Facilitate relapse prevention and coping; Advise on stop smoking medication; Ask about experiences of stop smoking medication that the smoker is using*
- Opportunity - *Advise on avoiding smoking cues by changing routine*
- Motivation - *Strengthen ex-smoker identity; Provide rewards contingent on successfully stopping smoking; Measure carbon monoxide to motivate abstinence*
- Adjuvant activities - *Give options for additional and later support*
- General support - *Elicit client views.*

Note that apart from BCTs that target motivation and capability BCTs were included that could help facilitate delivery of other BCTs.

Coding interventions using taxonomies of BCTs and linking mapping them to outcomes helps identify effective BCTs, demonstrates functions of BCTs associated with effective interventions and, when combined with other key information can provide evidence of the kinds of contexts in which BCTs are most effective.

Investigate the effectiveness of BCTs in evidence synthesis
Investigating the impact of specific BCTs on behaviour change has been conducted as part of evidence synthesis. Box 5.2 gives an example of how this has been done in a synthesis of audit and feedback interventions.

Box 5.2 Using BCT taxonomies in evidence synthesis

Using theory to synthesise evidence from behaviour change interventions: The example of audit and feedback [98, 99]

Background: Audit and feedback is regularly used as a method for improving professional practice. A Cochrane review of audit and feedback interventions [100] found modest and variable effects. As is the case for most evidence syntheses of behaviour change interventions, the content of interventions was not specified by BCTs and analyses were not guided by a theoretical understanding of the putative mechanisms of action of the interventions.

Aims: To re-analyse the Cochrane review of audit and feedback interventions [100] using BCTs to specify content and theory to guide analysis to organise, understand and synthesise evidence.

Methods: 61 reports of trials of audit and feedback interventions were characterised using the constructs of Control Theory (see [98]). Descriptions of interventions were coded for the presence of three BCTs linked to Control Theory: *feedback on current performance, setting behaviourally specific performance targets, and action plans* to implement to reduce any discrepancies observed between target and observed practice. A multivariate meta-regression was conducted to investigate the effects of feedback on its own, feedback combined with explicit targets, and feedback and targets combined with action plans (Control Theory predicts increasing effectiveness of these combinations). Whilst there was not sufficient power in the 2006 review to test the theoretical hypothesis, the updated Cochrane review [99] used this analysis strategy.

Results: The updated Cochrane review found that interventions that added explicit targets and action plans to feedback were more effective than those that did not, supporting the theoretically based hypothesis and showing the benefit of using BCTs and theory to guide evidence synthesis.

2. Investigate the functions played by BCTs

BCTs identified in interventions can be described in terms of the functions they play, as shown in Table 3.3 (p151) which links BCTs in BCTTv1 to intervention functions of the BCW. To illustrate how intervention content can be specified by BCT and intervention function, Table 5.2 shows how the three motivational and three self-regulatory BCTs identified as frequently occurring in the effective Txt2Stop intervention for smoking cessation [96]. In this case, the intervention functions of the motivational BCTs are 'education', 'persuasion' and 'environmental restructuring' and the function of the self-regulatory BCTs is 'enablement'.

Table 5.2 Linking BCTs in the Txt2Stop intervention to intervention functions

BCTs used in Txt2Stop	BCTs in BCT Taxonomy (v1)	Intervention function
Motivational:		
Provide information on consequences of smoking and smoking cessation	Information about social and environmental consequences Information about health consequences Information about emotional consequences	Education Persuasion
Boost motivation and self-efficacy Create or reinforce negative associations	Verbal persuasion about capability Associative learning	Persuasion Enablement Environmental restructuring
Self-regulatory:		
Promote use of relaxation techniques	Body changes	Enablement
Promote behavioural substitution	Behaviour substitution	Enablement
Provide behavioural substitution	Behaviour substitution	Enablement

Box 5.3 Using BCW in evidence synthesis

Using the BCW to synthesise evidence: The example of interventions to promote adherence to medications aimed at lowering cardiovascular disease risk [101]

Aim: To determine the effects of interventions (sometimes referred to as strategies) to improve adherence to CVD-related medications in socioeconomically disadvantaged groups.

Method: 14 randomised/quasi-randomised controlled trials. Studies were thematically grouped according to the intervention's target: patients, physician/practices, or both.

They were then coded according to the nine BCW intervention functions (education, persuasion, incentivisation, enablement, training, coercion, restriction, environmental restructuring, and modelling) and the seven policy categories (communication/ marketing, guidelines, fiscal, regulation, legislation, environmental/social planning, and service provision).

Results: Relative to patient- or physician/practice-only interventions, those simultaneously directed at patients and physicians/practices statistically significantly improved relative adherence (16–169%).

Education and enablement were the most common intervention functions; these were frequently supported by service provision and policies that incorporated guidelines to either mandate or recommend practice, as well as using various media for communication. The following were not included: patient incentivisation, coercive measures, legislative or fiscal policies, or changes in the broader physical or social environment.

Conclusion: Effective strategies to improve adherence in disadvantaged groups were generally complex: simultaneously targeting patients and physicians; addressing social, financial, and treatment-related adherence barriers; and supported by broader guidelines, regulatory and communication-based policies.

3. Specify theoretical underpinnings of interventions and understand processes of change

This section shows how the tools used in intervention design in Chapters 1-3 can also be applied to specify the theoretical principles on which interventions are based and to understand the processes of change.

Using BCT taxonomies to specify theoretical underpinnings of intervention components

Coding intervention content using BCT taxonomies and linking to mechanisms of action allows one to conduct mediational analyses to test hypotheses about the theoretical underpinning of interventions. This can be done both in evidence syntheses (see Box 5.3, p214) and in primary studies. An example of the latter is illustrated for an internet-based smoking cessation intervention, StopAdvisor [88]. A selection of BCTs and the theoretical principles to which they are linked are shown in Table 5.3.

Table 5.3 Linking theoretical principles to BCTs and intervention components in the design of StopAdvisor

Theoretical principle [8]	BCT [9]	Intervention component
Construct personal rule to generate strong resolve.	Prompt commitment from the client there and then; Strengthen ex-smoker identity; Explain importance of abrupt cessation.	Text encouraging users to repeat to themselves: 'Smoking is not an option'. Explain and introduce a motto: 'Not a puff — no matter what' and an image to accompany this.
Develop new, and maximise impact of existing, sources of desire not to smoke.	Provide normative information about others' behaviour and experiences; Build general rapport; Provide information on withdrawal symptoms; Provide reassurance.	Text offers reassurance and suggests high craving are a normal part of quitting smoking
Avoid cues that trigger urges to smoke.	Advise on changing routines.	Users will be advised that there are some daily routines that can trigger cravings, and suggested changes to those routines will be recommended.
Develop effective ways of distracting attention.	Facilitate relapse prevention and coping.	A section will explain the potential benefits of using glucose tablets to suppress cravings.

[8] PRIME theory of motivation informed development of StopAdvisor [19] www.primetheory.com

[9] A taxonomy of BCTs used in behavioural support for smoking cessation was used to develop the StopAdvisor intervention and differs from the taxonomy described in Chapter 2.

Being explicit about these links allows one to use experimental designs to improve the intervention by adding, substituting or varying the intensity or nature of components. For example, the intervention component in the table above 'text offers reassurance and suggests high craving are a normal part of quitting smoking' could be evaluated by being present or absent in different versions of the intervention or be low intensity (e.g. sent once a week) or high intensity (e.g. sent four times a day). Collins and colleagues (the MOST approach; [102]) propose an experimental paradigm that tests the effectiveness of combinations of BCTs. They use fractional factorial designs, drawing on both theory and accumulated evidence, as a basis for optimising intervention effectiveness. These methods have the advantage that they not only provide evidence of effective combinations, but also they efficiently test theoretical propositions about the synergy of BCTs.

Using COM-B and TDF to understand processes of change
Tools such as the COM-B model and TDF can be used to understand behaviour as a first point in intervention design. They can also be applied to specify mediators of behaviour change when planning evaluations of interventions. This enables evaluations to not only investigate whether behaviour has changed but also the mechanism by which any change have come about. Box 5.4 summarises how COM-B and TDF have been used to specify mediators of behaviour change in planning an evaluation of an internet intervention to promote condom use.

Box 5.4 Using COM-B and TDF to understand change processes

Using COM-B and TDF to select mediators of behaviour change in an intervention to promote condom use in men [103]

Aims: To use COM-B and TDF to identify and select mediators of change in condom use in an intervention to promote condom use in men and specify how they will be measured.

Methods: Literature reviews, interviews with men and consultations with experts in the area of sexual health were conducted to identify barriers and facilitators to men's condom use. Identified barriers and facilitators were mapped to COM-B components and TDF domains.

Results: Self-reported condom use after three months was the primary outcome measure. All COM-B components and most TDF domains were represented in mediators selected for measurement. These are summarised in Table 5.4 together with methods of measurement or, in the case of unselected domains, reasons non-selection.

Table 5.4 Mediators linked to TDF and COM-B

COM-B component	TDF domain	Mediator
Physical capability	Physical skills	Self-reported errors and problems with condoms, failure to use condoms due to being under the influence of alcohol or drugs.
Psychological capability	Knowledge	Knowledge of STI risk, knowledge of condom sizes and types, self-reported errors and problems with condoms.
	Cognitive and interpersonal skills	Communication with partners, self-efficacy for negotiating condom use.
	Memory, attention and decision processes	Not targeted by the intervention so not measured as a mediator.
	Behavioural regulation	Not selected as an intervention component so not measured as a mediator.
Reflective motivation	Professional/ social role and identity	Identity associated with condom use (e.g. responsible, manly).
	Beliefs about capabilities	Self-efficacy in applying condoms and negotiating condom use.
	Optimism	*Not targeted by the intervention so not measured as a mediator.*
	Beliefs about consequences	Beliefs about how condoms impact upon pleasure, evaluation of condom use (i.e. do the costs outweigh the benefits), knowledge of STI risk.
	Intentions	Intention to use condoms.
	Goals	*Whilst the intervention website asks participants to set goals related to condom use; the research team considered goals to be a mechanism by which behaviour change occurs, and so were not measured as a mediator.*

Table continued.

Automatic motivation	Reinforcement	*Not targeted by the intervention so not measured as a mediator.*
	Emotion	*Not targeted by the intervention so not measured as a mediator.*
Physical opportunity	Environmental context and resources	'Not having condoms available when needed' assessed within self-reported errors and problems.
Social opportunity	Social influences	*The intervention website gives examples of positive women's views on condom use, and men suggesting condom use; however, norms regarding condom use are relatively low, and so it was not though appropriate to give information about this within the intervention. Norms were not the primary focus of the intervention. Perception of norms will therefore not be measured as a mediator.*

4. Assess fidelity of delivery

Fidelity of delivery refers to the extent to which an intervention is delivered as planned (as outlined in the intervention protocol). If an intervention that has been shown to be effective in research trials is not implemented as planned, we do not know what is being evaluated. Intervention fidelity should therefore be assessed and reported, as recommended in both the MRC framework for developing and evaluating complex interventions [11] and in the CONSORT statement for reporting randomised controlled trials [104].

Not measuring fidelity when evaluating interventions can lead to spurious results. For example, accounting for intervention fidelity in a trial comparing an intervention of secondary care teleconsultations with standard outpatient care removed the previously reported association [105] between teleconsultation and increased outpatient follow-up [106].

So how can tools that support the design of interventions to change behaviour help us to determine how well interventions are delivered? One example is the use of BCT taxonomies. As described earlier, these provide a consistent language to describe intervention content. By specifying each BCT in study protocols or intervention manuals, we can determine whether they are delivered in the trial or real-world setting. A reliable method for identifying fidelity of delivery of behavioural support for smoking cessation has been developed using BCT methodology [97, 107]. Box 5.5 gives an example of how this has been done in English Stop Smoking Services.

221

By coding interventions in this way, it is possible to determine which of the planned BCTs were delivered, which were not, and whether any additional BCTs were delivered (i.e. not specified in intervention protocol or manual but delivered in practice). Identifying which BCTs are not delivered is the first step in improving fidelity. The next step is to understand why techniques are not delivered. As we have seen, tools such as the COM-B and TDF can support this.

Box 5.5 Using BCT taxonomies to assess fidelity of intervention delivery

Assessing fidelity of delivery of smoking cessation behavioural support in practice [97]

Aims: To assess fidelity of delivery of behavioural support in two English Stop-Smoking Services

Methods: Transcripts of audio-recorded behavioural support sessions and treatment manuals from two English Stop-Smoking Services were coded using a taxonomy of BCTs used in smoking cessation. Fidelity was determined by calculating the proportion of BCTs identified in the treatment manual that were identified in the behavioural support session transcripts. Additional information on when the session took place and the practitioner were also collected.

Results: 66% of BCTs identified in treatment manuals were identified in the delivery of behavioural support sessions. This indicates that around a third of planned content was not delivered. Over half of the BCTs delivered were not specified by the manual. The researchers were also able to identify variations in levels of fidelity over time. For example, fidelity was highest in sessions before the quit date in one service but lowest at this point in the other.

5. Evaluate other behaviour change frameworks

The BCW was developed to meet three criteria not met by the 19 frameworks of behaviour change identified in a systematic literature review. The criteria were comprehensiveness, coherence, and being linked to a model of behaviour. From this point of view, the BCW can be used as a benchmark against which to evaluate other frameworks.

Here we show a worked example of using the BCW to evaluate a framework, the Individual, Social and Material (ISM) model [108] which was identified after the development of the BCW and first used in work for the Scottish Government to examine the effectiveness of low carbon behaviour change interventions [109].

Summary of the Individual, Social and Material (ISM) model [108]
The Individual, Social and Material (ISM) model forms the basis of the ISM tool – intended to be a practical device for designing behaviour change interventions to bring about social change. According to the authors the model combines 'the most pertinent factors and influences from multiple disciplines, in order to provide a practical tool for policy makers, practitioners and researchers.' The model draws on the principles of behavioural economics, social psychology and sociology.

Three contexts comprising several factors make up the model: Individual - factors held by the individual that affect the choices and behaviours they undertake (including: values, beliefs, attitudes; costs & benefits; emotions; agency; skills; habit); Social - factors that exist beyond the individual in the social realm, yet shape their behaviours (including opinion leaders; institutions; norms; roles and identity; tastes; meanings; networks & relationships) and Material - factors that are 'out there' in the environment and wider world, which both constrain and shape behaviour (including rules and regulations; technologies infrastructure; objects; time and schedules). Definitions of these factors and the context to which they belong are given in Table 5.5. By comparison with the BCW, we can evaluate the ISM model on comprehensiveness, coherence and link to a model of behaviour

Comprehensiveness of the ISM model:
To assess the relative comprehensiveness of the ISM model and BCW, factors comprising the ISM model were coded according to components of the COM-B model, intervention functions and policy categories of the BCW (Table 5.5). This exercise demonstrated that the ISM describes factors that are covered by the COM-B model but does not include interventions and policies, with the exception of 'Rules and regulations'. Thus, it leaves the process of determining how to achieve change to the user.

Table 5.5 Linking factors of the ISM model to the Behaviour Change Wheel

Behaviour Change Wheel	The ISM model
COM-B model components	
Physical capability Physical skill	No ISM factors were coded to this COM-B component
Psychological capability The capacity to engage in the necessary thought processes - comprehension, reasoning	**Skills** - the things a person needs to know in order to carry out a behaviour. These include both procedural knowledge ('know how') and factual knowledge ('know what') (Individual)
Reflective motivation Reflective processes, involving evaluations and plans	**Cost/benefits** - calculation is the basic method of decision making, in which the perceived benefits (or 'utility') of acting are weighed against the perceived costs of doing so, including non-monetary costs such as time. However recent research has shown that much of this decision making is based on mental shortcuts, which can introduce errors, rather than effortful calculations (Individual)
	Agency – self-control and a person's confidence that they can undertake the behaviour in question, and see it through to completion. It usually relates to a specific object or situation, but people can also be described as 'low agency' (generally lacking in confidence) (Individual)
	Roles and Identity – roles relate to a person's different repertoires of behaviours and attitudes, based on the 'role' they are fulfilling at the time (mother, employee, football supporter etc.). The related concept of identity is a person's innate sense of who they are (Social) **Values** - part of the basic elements of an individual's motivational system: the most abstract and broad-based (Individual)
	Beliefs - part of the basic elements of an individual's motivational system: particular worldviews (Individual)
	Attitudes - part of the basic elements of an individual's motivational system: their views on specific things such as objects, activities or other people (Individual)

Automatic motivation Automatic processes involving emotions and impulses that arise from associative learning and/or innate dispositions	**Emotions** - how people feel about something – their emotional response –is one aspect in their behavioural decision-making (Individual) **Habit** - behaviours which are undertaken automatically and frequently, with little conscious thought, and usually in the same time or place. These can also be understood as routines (Individual)
Physical opportunity Opportunity afforded by the environment	**Infrastructure** - hard infrastructure relates to the firm boundaries to people's behavioural choices presented by the environments in which they live (for example, without a bus service, there will be no chance of bus use). Such factors can often prevent even motivated people from undertaking the behaviour in question. Alongside hard infrastructure, soft infrastructure emphasises features of everyday life which also bound individual action, but are not concrete - see Time & Schedules, and Rules & Regulations (Material) **Objects** - many behaviours (e.g. cycling to work) involve the use of objects (e.g. a bike, cycle racks at work), and the lack of necessary objects can stop a practice from being undertaken. As with technologies, objects and individual users interact such that sometimes the object can 'act back' on its owners and heavily influence how much time an individual spends on which practices (Context) **Time and schedules** - time is a finite resource that gets used in the course of carrying out everyday activities. Like money, it is a scarce resource that people have to allocate across competing demands (Material)

Table continued.

Social opportunity Opportunity afforded by the cultural milieu that dictates the way that we think about things (e.g. the words and concepts that make up our language)	**Norms** - people's perception of how other people (especially 'significant' others) would view their behaviour. In turn these perceptions have a strong influence on the behavioural decisions that people make (Social) **Tastes** - preferences through which people signal their belonging to particular social groups, e.g. kinds of music listened to, or table manners. These preferences are collectively developed and are based on shared understandings of appropriate and desirable conduct (Social) **Meanings** - culturally-constructed understandings of daily life which can include images, ideas, metaphors, and associations. These meanings effectively set the frame for a behaviour or practice, and in so doing so influence how it is undertaken, and how it is understood, e.g. smoking in popular culture used to mean sophistication and glamour, but now is more likely to mean an unhealthy lifestyle (Social) **Opinion Leaders** - individuals who have a strong influence over others for instance in shaping social norms (Social) **Institutions** - institutions influence how groups of individuals behave when they are engaging in particular activities or interacting with other people. Institutions can be formal such as the legal system or more informal such as family life (Social) **Networks and relationships** - connections between individuals, which people draw upon in identifying and carrying out possible courses of action (this is sometimes called 'social capital'). In aggregate, social networks can help to explain how ideas, innovations and behaviours can spread (Social)

Intervention functions	
Education Increasing knowledge or understanding	No ISM factors were coded to this intervention function
Persuasion Using communication to induce positive or negative feelings or stimulate action	No ISM factors were coded to this intervention function
Incentivisation Creating an expectation of reward	No ISM factors were coded to this intervention function
Coercion Creating an expectation of punishment or cost	No ISM factors were coded to this intervention function
Training Imparting skills	No ISM factors were coded to this intervention function
Restriction Using rules to reduce the opportunity to engage in the target behaviour (or to increase the target behaviour by reducing the opportunity to engage in competing behaviours)	Rules and regulations - set out by formal institutions, such as government, to prescribe or prohibit certain kinds of behaviour (e.g. through the taxation system). Yet rules and regulations are also implicit, for instance determining appropriate conduct for individuals in informal institutions (Material)
Environmental restructuring Changing the physical or social context	No ISM factors were coded to this intervention function
Modelling Providing an example for people to aspire to or imitate	No ISM factors were coded to this intervention function

Table continued.

Enablement Increasing means/ reducing barriers to increase capability (beyond education and training) or opportunity (beyond environmental restructuring)	No ISM factors were coded to this intervention function
Policy categories	
Communication/ marketing Using print, electronic, telephonic or broadcast media	No ISM factors were coded to this category
Guidelines Creating documents that recommend or mandate practice - this includes all changes to service provision	No ISM factors were coded to this category
Fiscal measures Using the tax system to reduce or increase the financial cost	No ISM factors were coded to this category
Regulation Establishing rules or principles of behaviour or practice	**Rules and regulations** - set out by formal institutions, such as government, to prescribe or prohibit certain kinds of behaviour (e.g. through the taxation system). Yet rules and regulations are also implicit, for instance determining appropriate conduct for individuals in informal institutions (Material)
Legislation Making or changing laws	**Rules and regulations** - At their most basic, rules and regulations are set out by formal institutions, such as government, to prescribe or prohibit certain kinds of behaviour (e.g. through the taxation system). Yet rules and regulations are also implicit, for instance determining appropriate conduct for individuals in informal institutions (Material)

Environmental/social planning Designing and/or controlling the physical or social environment	No ISM factors were coded to this category
Service provision Delivering a service	No ISM factors were coded to this category

Coherence of the ISM model:
The model could not be considered coherent as mode of delivery (e.g. technologies) is mixed together with behavioural explanatory factors (e.g. attitudes) and factors describing how behaviour might be changed (e.g. rules and regulations).

For example, 'technologies' is included under the context 'material' but appears to describe a mode of delivery by which interventions to change behaviour could be delivered rather than describing how behaviour change could be brought about: 'Technology' is sometimes contrasted to behaviour, in that techno-fixes are presented as ruling out the need for individuals to change their behaviour. However, individuals and technologies interact, and this can influence the effectiveness of a technology in terms of its desired impact (e.g. smart meters and how they are used in practice). This interaction also enables new practices, and the meanings of these practices, to spring up and take hold quickly (e.g. tweeting).

One can use the BCW to describe intervention functions and their associated BCTs: for example, smart meters can be thought of as environmental restructuring, bringing about change by providing the BCTs of feedback on behaviour.

Link to a model of behaviour:
Whilst the Individual, Social and Material (ISM) model draws on the disciplines of behavioural economics, social psychology and sociology there does not appear to be any explicit links to models or theories of behaviour.

Conclusion
The ISM model focuses on factors that influence behaviour plus a single type of policy lever, 'rules and regulations' (which conflates legislative and non-legislative measures). It also contains one mode of delivery, 'technologies'.

Linking the factors comprising the ISM model to the BCW highlights the fact that the ISM model does not include intervention functions or most policy levers, namely: intervention functions of education, persuasion, incentivisation, coercion, training, environmental restructuring, modelling and enablement; and policy categories of communication/marketing, guidelines, fiscal measures, environmental/social planning and service provision.

Addendum: Using formal theories to design and evaluate behaviour change interventions

For each intervention function of the BCW or domain of the TDF, there are a number of formal theories that may be valuable in intervention design and evaluation. For example, if 'perceived capability' was identified as an explanation for current behaviour, Social Cognitive Theory [110] would be a relevant theory to guide intervention design. A cross-disciplinary project, drawing on psychology, sociology, anthropology and economics, has identified 83 theories of behaviour change (http://www.ucl.ac.uk/health-psychology/research-group/research_themes/theories_and_techniques.php). Expertise is required to evaluate theories and select them for particular purposes, and to apply them to intervention development and evaluation. ABC of Behaviour Change Theories [12], a companion to the current guide, will provide summaries of the 83 theories, list their component constructs and provide some guidance to their use.

For more information and to obtain a copy of the book go to www.behaviourchangetheories.com.

Glossary

Behaviour: Anything a person does in response to internal or external events. Actions may be overt and directly measurable, or covert and indirectly measurable; behaviours are physical events that occur in the body and are controlled by the brain.

Behaviour pattern: A type of behaviour that is repeated and can be described in terms of its frequency of occurrence or other aggregate measures (e.g. smoking, alcohol consumption, exceeding the speed limit, overeating).

Behaviour Change Intervention: An activity or co-ordinated set of activities that aims to get an individual or population to behave differently from how s/he or they would have acted without such an action.

Behaviour Change Technique: An active component of an intervention designed to change behaviour. The defining characteristics of a BCT are that it is observable, replicable, irreducible, a component of an intervention designed to change behaviour and a postulated active ingredient within the intervention. It is thus the smallest component compatible with retaining the postulated active ingredients, i.e. the proposed mechanisms of change, and can be used alone or in combination with other BCTs.

COM-B model: A model comprised of three components - Capability, Opportunity and Motivation - that are necessary for a given behaviour to occur; it provides a simple approach to understanding behaviour in context.

Framework: A conceptual scheme.

Implementation: Putting into effect.

Intervention function: Functions served by an intervention targeting factors that influence behaviour. In the BCW these are defined broadly on the basis of labels and descriptors previously used in the literature.

Model: A specification of a set of elements or constructs and inter-relations between them that represent an object or system in the world outside of itself. It can be used to predict, explain or simply describe a set of events or phenomena.

Target behaviour: The behaviour targeted either for change (in the context of intervention design) or to be understood (in the context of understanding an implementation problem).

Taxonomy: A classification of constructs (e.g. objects, events, characteristics, processes etc.), typically involving hierarchical associations between categories.

Theoretical Domains Framework: A synthesis of constructs from behaviour change theories, developed in a consensus process to make theories more accessible for implementation and behaviour change researchers.

Theory: A model or set of models that aims to explain and predict phenomena.

Links to other resources

1. UCL Centre for Behaviour Change
   http://www.ucl.ac.uk/behaviour-change

2. BCT Taxonomy website
   www.ucl.ac.uk/health-psychology/BCTtaxonomy

3. NICE Public Health Guidance on Behaviour Change:
   Individual Approaches (PH49)
   http://guidance.nice.org.uk/PH49

4. Cochrane Library
   http://www.thecochranelibrary.com

5. UK Society for Behavioural Medicine
   http://uksbm.org.uk

6. National Centre for Smoking Cessation and Training
   www.ncsct.co.uk

Appendix 1: Behaviour change frameworks contributing to the Behaviour Change Wheel

1. **Epicure taxonomy** [20] Taxonomy of approaches designed to influence behaviour patterns

2. **Culture capital framework** [111] Framework of knowledge about culture change, offering practical tools for policymaking

3. **EPOC taxonomy of interventions** Cochrane Effective Practice and Organisation of Care Review Group (EPOC) [112] Checklist to guide systematic literature reviewers about the types of information to extract from primary studies

4. **RURU: Intervention implementation taxonomy** [113] Taxonomy covering a wide range of policy, practice and organisational targets aimed at increasing impact of research

5. **MINDSPACE** Institute for Government and Cabinet Office [13] Checklist for policy-makers aimed at changing or shaping behaviour

6. **Taxonomy of behaviour change techniques** [114] Taxonomy of behaviour change techniques grouped by change targets

237

7. **Intervention mapping** [14] Protocol for a systematic development of theory- and evidence-based interventions

8. **People and places framework** [115] Framework that explains how communication and marketing can be used to advance public health

9. **Public health: ethical issues** [17] Ladder of interventions by government, industry, organisations and individuals to promote public health.

10. **Injury control framework** [116] Heuristic framework for categorising and evaluating behaviour change strategies aimed at controlling injuries

11. **Implementation taxonomy** [4] Theory-based taxonomy of methods for implementing change in practice

12. **Legal framework** [117] Conceptual framework for identifying possible legal strategies used for preventing cardiovascular diseases

13. **PETeR White** [118] Comprehensive and universally applicable model or taxonomy of health

14. **DEFRA's 4E model** [119] Process model for policy makers aimed at promoting pro-environmental behaviours in accordance with social marketing principles

15. **STD/ HIV framework** [120] Taxonomy to expand the scope of interventions that can be used to prevent STD and HIV transmission

16. **Framework on public policy in physical activity** [121] Taxonomy aimed at understanding how and why policies successfully impact on behaviour change

17. **Intervention framework for retail pharmacies** [122] A framework that presents factors that may affect retail pharmacy describing and strategies for behaviour change to improve appropriateness of prescribing

18. **Environmental policy framework** [123] A taxonomy of major environmental problems, their different levels and global spheres of impact, and conceptual modelling of environmental problem-solving

19. **Population Services International (PSI) framework** [124] A conceptual framework to guide and help conduct research on social marketing interventions

Appendix 2: Worksheets

Worksheet 1 – Define the problem in behavioural terms

This Worksheet allows you to set out in behavioural terms the problem you are trying to solve and the individual, group or population involved.

What behaviour?	
Where does the behaviour occur?	
Who is involved in performing the behaviour?	

Worksheet 2 – Select the target behaviour

Task 1: Generate a long list of candidate target behaviours that could bring about the desired outcome

Intervention designer response

Task 2: Prioritise the behaviours by considering the following criteria:

1. How much of an impact changing the behaviour will have on desired outcome
2. How likely it is that the behaviour can be changed (when considering likelihood of change being achieved, think about the capability, opportunity and motivation to change of those performing the behaviour)
3. How likely it is that the behaviour (or group of behaviours) will have a positive or negative impact on other, related behaviours
4. How easy it will be to measure the behaviour

Different criteria will be more or less important in different situations. As a result of this prioritization exercise, you are likely to reach one of the following decisions:

1. The behaviour appears very promising as a target behaviour
2. The behaviour is quite promising as a target behaviour
3. The behaviour appears unpromising but is worth considering as a target behaviour
4. The behaviour is not acceptable as the target behaviour (it doesn't matter what it is like on the other criteria, this behaviour cannot be selected as the intervention target)

Potential target behaviours	Impact of behaviour change (unacceptable, unpromising but worth considering, promising, very promising)	Likelihood of changing behaviour (unacceptable, unpromising but worth considering, promising, very promising)	Spillover score (unacceptable, unpromising but worth considering, promising, very promising)	Measurement score (unacceptable, unpromising but worth considering, promising, very promising)
Record selected target behaviour here:				

Worksheet 3 – Specify the target behaviour

Task: Describe the target behaviour according to who, needs to do what, when, where, how often and with whom

Target behaviour	
Who **needs to perform the behaviour?**	
What **do they need to do differently to achieve the desired change?**	
When **do they need to do it?**	
Where **do they need to do it?**	
How often **do they need to do it?**	
With whom **do they need to do it?**	

Worksheet 4 – Identify what needs to change

Task: Use the COM-B model to identify what needs to change in order for the target behaviour to occur:

COM-B Components	What needs to happen for the target behaviour to occur?	Is there a need for change?
Physical capability		
Psychological capability		
Physical opportunity		
Social opportunity		
Reflective motivation		
Automatic motivation		
Behavioural diagnosis of the relevant COM-B components:		

Worksheet 4a – Identify what needs to change using the TDF

Task: If a more detailed understanding of the behaviour is required, use the TDF to expand on COM-B components identified in the behavioural diagnosis.

COM-B	TDF	Relevance of domain
Physical capability	Physical skills	
Psychological capability	Knowledge	
	Cognitive and interpersonal skills	
	Memory, attention and decision processes	
	Behavioural regulation	
Physical opportunity	Environmental context and resources	
Social opportunity	Social influences	
Reflective motivation	Professional/social role and identity	
	Beliefs about capabilities	
	Optimism	
	Beliefs about consequences	
	Intentions	
	Goals	
Automatic motivation	Reinforcement	
	Emotion	

Worksheet 5 – Identify intervention functions

Task: Use the APEASE criteria to identify appropriate intervention functions based on the behavioural diagnosis arrived at in Step 4(4a):

- Affordability
- Practicability
- Effectiveness and cost-effectiveness
- Acceptability
- Side-effects/safety
- Equity

Candidate intervention functions	Does the intervention function meet the APEASE criteria (affordability, practicability, effectiveness/cost-effectiveness, acceptability, side-effects/safety, equity)?
Education	
Persuasion	
Incentivisation	
Coercion	
Training	
Restriction	
Environmental restructuring	
Modelling	
Enablement	
Selected intervention functions:	

Worksheet 6 – Identify policy categories

Task: Use the APEASE criteria to identify appropriate policy categories based on the intervention functions identified in Step 5:

- Affordability
- Practicability
- Effectiveness and cost-effectiveness
- Acceptability
- Side-effects/safety
- Equity

Intervention function	Policy categories	Does the policy category meet the APEASE criteria (affordability, practicability, effectiveness/cost-effectiveness, acceptability, side-effects/safety, equity)?
Education	Communication/ marketing Guidelines Regulation Legislation Service provision	
Persuasion	Communication/ marketing Guidelines Regulation Legislation Service provision	
Incentivisation	Communication/ marketing Guidelines Fiscal measures Regulation Legislation Service provision	

Coercion	Communication/ marketing Guidelines Fiscal measures Regulation Legislation Service provision	
Training	Guidelines Fiscal measures Regulation Legislation Service provision	
Restriction	Guidelines Regulation Legislation	
Environmental restructuring	Guidelines Fiscal measures Regulation Legislation Environmental/social planning	
Modelling	Communication/ marketing Service provision	
Enablement	Guidelines Fiscal measures Regulation Legislation Environmental/social planning Service provision	

Worksheet 7 – Identify BCTs

Task: Use the APEASE criteria to identify appropriate BCTs
based on the intervention functions identified in Step 5:

- Affordability
- Practicability
- Effectiveness and cost-effectiveness
- Acceptability
- Side-effects/safety
- Equity

Inter-vention function	Individual BCTs	Does the BCT meet the APEASE criteria (affordability, prac-ticability, effective-ness/cost-effective-ness, acceptability, side-effects/safety, equity)?
Educa-tion	**Most frequently used BCTs:** Information about social and environmental consequences Information about health consequences Feedback on behaviour Feedback on outcome(s) of the behaviour Prompts/cues Self-monitoring of behaviour Less frequently used BCTs: Biofeedback Self-monitoring of outcome(s) of behaviour Cue signalling reward Satiation Information about antecedents Re-attribution Behavioural experiments Information about emotional consequences Information about others' approval	

Persua-sion	**Most frequently used BCTs:** **Credible source** **Information about social and environmental consequences** **Information about health consequences** **Feedback on behaviour** **Feedback on outcome(s) of the behaviour** Less frequently used BCTs: Biofeedback Re-attribution Focus on past success Verbal persuasion about capability Framing/reframing Identity associated with changed behaviour Identification of self as role model Information about emotional consequences Salience of consequences Information about others' approval Social comparison	
Incentiv-isation	**Most frequently used BCTs:** **Feedback on behaviour** **Feedback on outcome(s) of behaviour** **Monitoring of behaviour by others without evidence of feedback** **Monitoring outcome of behaviour by others without evidence of feedback** **Self-monitoring of behaviour** Less frequently used BCTs: Paradoxical instructions Biofeedback Self-monitoring of outcome(s) of behaviour Cue signalling reward Remove aversive stimulus Reward approximation Rewarding completion Situation-specify reward Reward incompatible behaviour Reduce reward frequency Reward alternate behaviour Remove punishment Social reward Material reward Material reward (outcome) Self-reward Non-specific reward Incentive Behavioural contract Commitment Discrepancy between current behaviour and goal Imaginary reward	

251

Table continued.

Coercion	Most frequently used BCTs: Feedback on behaviour Feedback on outcome(s) of behaviour Monitoring of behaviour by others without evidence of feedback Monitoring outcome of behaviour by others without evidence of feedback Self-monitoring of behaviour Less frequently used BCTs: Biofeedback Self-monitoring of outcome(s) of behaviour Remove access to the reward Punishment Behaviour cost Remove reward Future punishment Behavioural contract Commitment Discrepancy between current behaviour and goal Incompatible beliefs Anticipated regret Imaginary punishment	
Training	Most frequently used BCTs: Demonstration of the behaviour Instruction on how to perform a behaviour Feedback on the behaviour Feedback on outcome(s) of behaviour Self-monitoring of behaviour Behavioural practice/rehearsal Less frequently used BCTs: Biofeedback Self-monitoring of outcome(s) of behaviour Habit formation Habit reversal Graded tasks Behavioural experiments Mental rehearsal of successful performance Self-talk Self-reward	
Restriction	No BCTs in BCTTv1 are linked to this intervention function because they are focused on changing the way that people think, feel and react rather than the way the external environment limits their behaviour.	

Environmental restructuring	**Most frequently used BCTs:** **Adding objects to the environment** **Prompts/cues** **Restructuring the physical environment** Less frequently used BCTs: Cue signalling reward Remove access to the reward Remove aversive stimulus Satiation Exposure Associative learning Reduce prompt/cue Restructuring the social environment	
Modelling	Most frequently used BCTs: Demonstration of the behaviour	

Table continued.

Enable-ment	Most frequently used BCTs: Social support (unspecified) Social support (practical) Goal setting (behaviour) Goal setting (outcome) Adding objects to the environment Problem solving Action planning Self-monitoring of behaviour Restructuring the physical environment Review behaviour goal(s) Review outcome goal(s) Less frequently used BCTs: Social support (emotional) Reduce negative emotions Conserve mental resources Pharmacological support Self-monitoring of outcome(s) of behaviour Behaviour substitution Overcorrection Generalisation of a target behaviour Graded tasks Avoidance/reducing exposure to cues for the behaviour Restructuring the social environment Distraction Body changes Behavioural experiments Mental rehearsal of successful performance Focus on past success Self-talk Verbal persuasion about capability Self-reward Behavioural contract Commitment Discrepancy between current behaviour and goal Pros and cons Comparative imagining of future outcomes Valued self-identity Framing/reframing Incompatible beliefs Identity associated with changed behaviour Identification of self as role model Salience of consequences Monitoring of emotional consequences Anticipated regret Imaginary punishment Imaginary reward Vicarious consequences	

Intervention function

Task: Based on the identified intervention functions, policy categories and BCTs, draft an intervention strategy describing how BCTs will be delivered in your context.

Intervention functions	COM-B components served by intervention functions	BCTs to deliver intervention functions	Policy categories through which BCTs can be delivered	Intervention strategy

Worksheet 8 – Identify mode of delivery

Task: Use the APEASE criteria to identify an appropriate mode of delivery:

- Affordability
- Practicability
- Effectiveness and cost-effectiveness
- Acceptability
- Side-effects/safety
- Equity

Mode of delivery				Does the mode of delivery meet the APEASE criteria (affordability, practicability, effectiveness/ cost-effectiveness, acceptability, side-effects/safety, equity)?
Face-to-face	Individual			
	Group			
Distance	Population-level	Broadcast media	TV	
			Radio	
		Outdoor media	Billboard	
			Poster	
		Print media	Newspaper	
			Leaflet	
		Digital media	Internet	
			Mobile phone app	
	Individual-level	Phone	Phone helpline	
			Mobile phone text	
		Individually accessed computer programme		

Appendix 3: Spin the Wheel Quiz - answers

1. Providing information on benefits of physical activity.

This is education as the aim is to increase knowledge about the impact of physical activity.

2. Fines for the possession of solvents.

This is coercion as there is a cost for the undesirable behaviour.

3. Creating a rewards system for GPs who ask about smoking behaviour.

This is incentivisation as there is a reward for the desirable behaviour.

4. Telling drinkers if they drink to excess they will be viewed negatively by their peers.

This is persuasion not coercion as there is no direct punishment or cost to the drinker.

5. A lecture about safe driving.

This is education as the aim is to impart knowledge, i.e. the what not the practical application of this knowledge, i.e. the how to that defines training.

6. Using TV advert to encourage condom use.

This is persuasion as the aim is to induce positive feelings towards condom use.

7. Providing cooking lessons.

This is training as the aim is to impart skill rather than increase knowledge.

8. Supporting GPs to recognise the symptoms ovarian cancer with an information pamphlet.

This would be considered education as the primary aim is to inform rather than support.

9. Using positive images of non-smokers to encourage smokers to quit.

This is persuasion as there is no direct reward.

Appendix 4: Behaviour Change Technique Taxonomy (v1)[f]

No.	Label	Definition	Examples
1. Goals and planning			
1.1	*Goal setting (behaviour)*	Set or agree a goal defined in terms of the behaviour to be achieved *Note: only code [g] goal-setting if there is sufficient evidence that goal set as part of intervention; if goal unspecified or a behavioural outcome, code 1.3, Goal setting (outcome); if the goal defines a specific context, frequency, duration or intensity for the behaviour, also code 1.4, Action planning*	Agree a daily walking goal (e.g. 3 miles) with the person and reach agreement about the goal Set the goal of eating 5 pieces of fruit per day as specified in public health guidelines
1.2	*Problem solving*	Analyse , or prompt the person to analyse, factors influencing the behaviouzr and generate or select strategies that include overcoming barriers and/or increasing facilitators (includes *'Relapse Prevention' and 'Coping Planning'*) Note: barrier identification without solutions is not sufficient. If the BCT does not include analysing the behavioural problem, consider 12.3, Avoidance/changing exp*osure to cues for the behaviour, 12.1, Restructuring the physical environment, 12.2, Restructuring the social environment, or 11.2, Reduce negative emotions*	Identify specific triggers (e.g. being in a pub, feeling anxious) that generate the urge/want/need to drink and develop strategies for avoiding environmental triggers or for managing negative emotions, such as anxiety, that motivate drinking Prompt the patient to identify barriers preventing them from starting a new exercise regime e.g., lack of motivation, and discuss ways in which they could help overcome them e.g. going to the gym with a buddy
1.3	*Goal setting (outcome)*	Set or agree a goal defined in terms of a positive **outcome** of wanted behaviour *Note: only code guidelines if set as a goal in an intervention context; if goal is a behaviour, code 1.1, Goal setting (behaviour); if goal unspecified code 1.3, Goal setting (outcome)*	Set a weight loss goal (e.g. 0.5 kilogram over one week) as an outcome of changed eating patterns

1.4	Action planning	Prompt detailed planning of performance of the behaviour (must include at least one of context, frequency, duration and intensity). Context may be environmental (physical or social) or internal (physical, emotional or cognitive) (includes *'Implementation Intentions'*) Note: evidence of action planning does not necessarily imply goal setting, only code latter if sufficient evidence	Encourage a plan to carry condoms when going out socially at weekends Prompt planning the performance of a particular physical activity (e.g. running) at a particular time (e.g. before work) on certain days of the week
1.5	*Review behaviour goal(s)*	Review behaviour goal(s) jointly with the person and consider modifying goal(s) or behaviour change strategy in light of achievement. This may lead to re-setting the same goal, a small change in that goal or setting a new goal instead of (or in addition to) the first, or no change Note: if goal specified in terms of behaviour, code **1.5, Review behaviour goal(s)**, if goal unspecified, code **1.7, Review outcome goal(s)**; if discrepancy created consider also **1.6, Discrepancy between current behaviour and goal**	Examine how well a person's performance corresponds to agreed goals e.g. whether they consumed less than one unit of alcohol per day, and consider modifying future behavioural goals accordingly e.g. by increasing or decreasing alcohol target or changing type of alcohol consumed
1.6	*Discrepancy between current behaviour and goal*	Draw attention to discrepancies between a person's current behaviour (in terms of the form, frequency, duration, or intensity of that behaviour) and the person's previously set outcome goals, behavioural goals or action plans (goes beyond self-monitoring of behaviour) Note: if discomfort is created only code **13.3, Incompatible beliefs** and not **1.6, Discrepancy between current behaviour and goal;** if goals are modified, also code **1.5, Review behaviour goal(s)** and/or **1.7, Review outcome goal(s);** if feedback is provided, also code **2.2, Feedback on behaviour**	Point out that the recorded exercise fell short of the goal set

1.7	*Review outcome goal(s)*	Review outcome goal(s) jointly with the person and consider modifying goal(s) in light of achievement. This may lead to re-setting the same goal, a small change in that goal or setting a new goal instead of, or in addition to the first *Note: if goal specified in terms of behaviour, code 1.5, Review behaviour goal(s), if goal unspecified, code 1.7, Review outcome goal(s); if discrepancy created consider also 1.6, Discrepancy between current behaviour and goal*	Examine how much weight has been lost and consider modifying outcome goal(s) accordingly e.g. by increasing or decreasing subsequent weight loss targets
1.8	*Behavioural contract*	Create a written specification of the behaviour to be performed, agreed by the person, and witnessed by another *Note: also code 1.1, Goal setting (behaviour)*	Sign a contract with the person e.g. specifying that they will not drink alcohol for one week
1.9	*Commitment*	Ask the person to affirm or reaffirm statements indicating commitment to change the behaviour *Note: if defined in terms of the behaviour to be achieved also code 1.1, Goal setting (behaviour)*	Ask the person to use an 'I will' statement to affirm or reaffirm a strong commitment (i.e. using the words 'strongly', 'committed' or 'high priority') to start, continue or restart the attempt to take medication as prescribed
2. Feedback and monitoring			

2.1	Monitoring of behaviour by others without feedback	Observe or record behaviour with the person's knowledge as part of a behaviour change strategy Note: if monitoring is part of a data collection procedure rather than a strategy aimed at changing behaviour, do not code; if feedback given, code only **2.2, Feedback on behaviour**, and <u>not</u> **2.1, Monitoring of behaviour by others without feedback**; if monitoring outcome(s) code **2.5, Monitoring outcome(s) of behaviour by others without feedback**; if self-monitoring behaviour, code **2.3, Self-monitoring of behaviour**	Watch hand washing behaviours among health care staff and make notes on context, frequency and technique used
2.2	Feedback on behaviour	Monitor and provide informative or evaluative feedback on performance of the behaviour (e.g. form, frequency, duration, intensity) Note: if Biofeedback, code only **2.6, Biofeedback** and <u>not</u> **2.2, Feedback on behaviour**; if feedback is on outcome(s) of behaviour, code **2.7, Feedback on outcome(s) of behaviour**; if there is no clear evidence that feedback was given, code **2.1, Monitoring of behaviour by others without feedback**; if feedback on behaviour is evaluative e.g. praise, also code **10.4, Social reward**	Inform the person of how many steps they walked each day (as recorded on a pedometer) or how many calories they ate each day (based on a food consumption questionnaire).
2.3	Self-monitoring of behaviour	Establish a method for the person to monitor and record their behaviour(s) as part of a behaviour change strategy Note: if monitoring is part of a data collection procedure rather than a strategy aimed at changing behaviour, do not code; if monitoring of outcome of behaviour, code **2.4, Self-monitoring of outcome(s) of behaviour**; if monitoring is by someone else (without feedback), code **2.1, Monitoring of behaviour by others without feedback**	Ask the person to record daily, in a diary, whether they have brushed their teeth for at least two minutes before going to bed Give patient a pedometer and a form for recording daily total number of steps

2.4	*Self-mon-itoring of outcome(s) of behaviour*	Establish a method for the person to monitor and record the **outcome(s)** of their behaviour as part of a behaviour change strategy *Note: if monitoring is part of a data collection procedure rather than a strategy aimed at changing behaviour, do not code ; if monitoring behaviour, code 2.3,* **Self-monitoring of behaviour;** *if monitoring is by someone else (without feedback), code* **2.5, Monitoring outcome(s) of behaviour by others without feedback**	Ask the person to weigh themselves at the end of each day, over a two week period, and record their daily weight on a graph to increase exercise behaviours
2.5	*Monitoring outcome(s) of behaviour by others without feedback*	Observe or record outcomes of behaviour with the person's knowledge as part of a behaviour change strategy *Note: if monitoring is part of a data collection procedure rather than a strategy aimed at changing behaviour, do not code; if feedback given, code only* **2.7, Feedback on outcome(s) of behaviour;** *if monitoring behaviour code* **2.1, Monitoring of behaviour by others without feedback;** *if self-monitoring outcome(s), code* **2.4, Self-monitoring of outcome(s) of behaviour**	Record blood pressure, blood glucose, weight loss, or physical fitness
2.6	*Biofeedback*	Provide feedback about the body (e.g. physiological or biochemical state) using an external monitoring device as part of a behaviour change strategy *Note: if Biofeedback, code only* **2.6, Biofeedback** *and* <u>**not**</u> **2.2, Feedback on behaviour or 2.7, Feedback on outcome(s) of behaviour**	Inform the person of their blood pressure reading to improve adoption of health behaviours

2.7	Feedback on outcome(s) of behaviour	Monitor and provide feedback on the outcome of performance of the behaviour Note: if Biofeedback, code only 2.6, Biofeedback and not 2.7, Feedback on outcome(s) of behaviour; if feedback is on behaviour code 2.2, Feedback on behaviour; if there is no clear evidence that feedback was given code 2.5, Monitoring outcome(s) of behaviour by others without feedback; if feedback on behaviour is evaluative e.g. praise, also code 10.4, Social reward	Inform the person of how much weight they have lost following the implementation of a new exercise regime
3. Social support			
3.1	Social support (unspecified)	Advise on, arrange or provide social support (e.g. from friends, relatives, colleagues,' buddies' or staff) or non-contingent praise or reward for performance of the behaviour. It includes encouragement and counselling, but only when it is directed at the **behaviour** Note: attending a group class and/or mention of 'follow-up' does not necessarily apply this BCT, support must be explicitly mentioned; if practical, code 3.2, Social support (practical); if emotional, code 3.3, Social support (emotional) (includes '**Motivational interviewing**' and '**Cognitive Behavioural Therapy**')	Advise the person to call a 'buddy' when they experience an urge to smoke Arrange for a housemate to encourage continuation with the behaviour change programme Give information about a self-help group that offers support for the behaviour

3.2	*Social support (practical)*	Advise on, arrange, or provide **practical** help (*e.g. from friends, relatives, colleagues, 'buddies' or staff*) for performance of the behaviour Note: if emotional, code **3.3**, *Social support (emotional)*; if general or unspecified, code **3.1**, *Social support (unspecified)* If only restructuring the physical environment or adding objects to the environment, code **12.1**, *Restructuring the physical environment or* **12.5**, *Adding objects to the environment*; attending a group or class and/or mention of 'follow-up' does not necessarily apply this BCT, support must be explicitly mentioned.	Ask the partner of the patient to put their tablet on the breakfast tray so that the patient remembers to take it
3.3	*Social support (emotional)*	Advise on, arrange, or provide **emotional** social support (*e.g. from friends, relatives, colleagues, 'buddies' or staff*) for performance of the behaviour Note: if practical, code **3.2**, *Social support (practical)*; if unspecified, code **3.1**, *Social support (unspecified)*	Ask the patient to take a partner or friend with them to their colonoscopy appointment

4. Shaping knowledge

4.1	*Instruction on how to perform a behaviour*	Advise or agree on how to perform the behaviour (includes '**Skills training**') Note: when the person attends classes such as exercise or cookery, code **4.1**, *Instruction on how to perform the behaviour*, **8.1**, *Behavioural practice/rehearsal and* **6.1**, *Demonstration of the behaviour*	Advise the person how to put a condom on a model of a penis correctly
4.2	*Information about antecedents*	Provide information about antecedents (*e.g. social and environmental situations and events, emotions, cognitions*) that reliably predict performance of the behaviour	Advise to keep a record of snacking and of situations or events occurring prior to snacking

4.4	*Behavioural experiments*	Advise on how to identify and test hypotheses about the behaviour, its causes and consequences, by collecting and interpreting data	Ask a family physician to give evidence-based advice rather than prescribe antibiotics and to note whether the patients are grateful or annoyed

5. Natural consequences

5.1	*Information about health consequences*	Provide information (e.g. written, verbal, visual) about health consequences of performing the behaviour *Note: consequences can be for any target, not just the recipient(s) of the intervention; emphasising importance of consequences is not sufficient; if information about emotional consequences, code* **5.6, Information about emotional consequences**; *if about social, environmental or unspecified consequences code* **5.3, Information about social and environmental consequences**	Explain that not finishing a course of antibiotics can increase susceptibility to future infection Present the likelihood of contracting a sexually transmitted infection following unprotected sexual behaviour
5.2	*Salience of consequences*	Use methods specifically designed to emphasise the consequences of performing the behaviour with the aim of making them more memorable (goes beyond informing about consequences) *Note: if information about consequences, also code* **5.1, Information about health consequences, 5.6, Information about emotional consequences** *or* **5.3, Information about social and environmental consequences**	Produce cigarette packets showing pictures of health consequences e.g. diseased lungs, to highlight the dangers of continuing to smoke

5.3	*Information about social and environmental consequences*	Provide information (e.g. written, verbal, visual) about social and environmental consequences of performing the behaviour *Note: consequences can be for any target, not just the recipient(s) of the intervention; if information about health or consequences, code **5.1, Information about health consequences**; if about emotional consequences, code **5.6, Information about emotional consequences**; if unspecified, code **5.3, Information about social and environmental consequences***	Tell family physician about financial remuneration for conducting health screening Inform a smoker that the majority of people disapprove of smoking in public places
5.4	*Monitoring of emotional consequences*	Prompt assessment of **feelings** after attempts at performing the behaviour	Agree that the person will record how they feel after taking their daily walk
5.5	*Anticipated regret*	Induce or raise awareness of expectations of future regret about performance of the unwanted behaviour *Note: <u>not</u> including **5.6, Information about emotional consequences**; if suggests adoption of a perspective or new perspective in order to change cognitions also code **13.2, Framing/reframing***	Ask the person to assess the degree of regret they will feel if they do not quit smoking
5.6	*Information about emotional consequences*	Provide information (e.g. written, verbal, visual) about emotional consequences of performing the behaviour *Note: consequences can be related to emotional health disorders (e.g. depression, anxiety) and/or states of mind (e.g. low mood, stress); <u>not</u> including **5.5, Anticipated regret**; consequences can be for any target, not just the recipient(s) of the intervention; if information about health consequences code **5.1, Information about health consequences**; if about social, environmental or unspecified code **5.3, Information about social and environmental consequences***	Explain that quitting smoking increases happiness and life satisfaction

6. Comparison of behaviour

6.1	*Demonstration of the behaviour*	Provide an observable sample of the performance of the behaviour, directly in person or indirectly e.g. via film, pictures, for the person to aspire to or imitate (includes '**Modelling**'). Note: if advised to practice, <u>also</u> code, *8.1, Behavioural practice and rehearsal*; If provided with instructions on how to perform, <u>also</u> code 4.1, *Instruction on how to perform the behaviour*	Demonstrate to nurses how to raise the issue of excessive drinking with patients via a role-play exercise
6.2	*Social comparison*	Draw attention to others' performance to allow comparison with the person's own performance *Note: being in a group setting does not necessarily mean that social comparison is actually taking place*	Show the doctor the proportion of patients who were prescribed antibiotics for a common cold by other doctors and compare with their own data
6.3	*Information about others' approval*	Provide information about what other people think about the behaviour. The information clarifies whether others will like, approve or disapprove of what the person is doing or will do	Tell the staff at the hospital ward that staff at all other wards approve of washing their hands according to the guidelines

7. Associations

7.1	*Prompts/ cues*	Introduce or define environmental or social stimulus with the purpose of prompting or cueing the behaviour. The prompt or cue would normally occur at the time or place of performance *Note: when a stimulus is linked to a specific action in an if-then plan including one or more of frequency, duration or intensity* <u>also</u> *code 1.4, Action planning.*	Put a sticker on the bathroom mirror to remind people to brush their teeth

7.2	*Cue signal-ling reward*	Identify an environmental stimulus that reliably predicts that reward will follow the behaviour (includes '**Discriminative cue**')	Advise that a fee will be paid to dentists for a particular dental treatment of 6-8 year old, but not older, children to encourage delivery of that treatment (the 6-8 year old children are the environmental stimulus)
7.3	*Reduce prompts/ cues*	Withdraw gradually prompts to perform the behaviour (includes '**Fading**')	Reduce gradually the number of reminders used to take medication
7.4	*Remove access to the reward*	Advise or arrange for the person to be separated from situations in which unwanted behaviour can be rewarded in order to reduce the behaviour (includes '**Time out**')	Arrange for cupboard containing high calorie snacks to be locked for a specified period to reduce the consumption of sugary foods in between meals
7.5	*Remove aversive stimulus*	Advise or arrange for the removal of an aversive stimulus to facilitate behaviour change (includes '**Escape learning**')	Arrange for a gym-buddy to stop nagging the person to do more exercise in order to increase the desired exercise behaviour
7.6	*Satiation*	Advise or arrange repeated exposure to a stimulus that reduces or extinguishes a drive for the unwanted behaviour	Arrange for the person to eat large quantities of chocolate, in order to reduce the person's appetite for sweet foods
7.7	*Exposure*	Provide systematic confrontation with a feared stimulus to reduce the response to a later encounter	Agree a schedule by which the person who is frightened of surgery will visit the hospital where they are scheduled to have surgery

7.8	*Associative learning*	Present a neutral stimulus jointly with a stimulus that already elicits the behaviour repeatedly until the neutral stimulus elicits that behaviour (includes '**Classical/Pavlovian Conditioning**') *Note: when a BCT involves reward or punishment, code one or more of:* **10.2, Material reward** *(behaviour);* **10.3, Non-specific reward;** **10.4, Social reward,** **10.9, Self-reward;** **10.10, Reward** *(outcome)*	Present repeatedly fatty foods with a disliked sauce to discourage the consumption of fatty foods

8. Repetition and substitution

8.1	*Behavioural practice/ rehearsal*	Prompt practice or rehearsal of the performance of the behaviour one or more times in a context or at a time when the performance may not be necessary, in order to increase habit and skill *Note: if aiming to associate performance with the context, <u>also</u> code* **8.3, Habit formation**	Prompt asthma patients to practice measuring their peak flow in the nurse's consulting room
8.2	*Behaviour substitution*	Prompt substitution of the unwanted behaviour with a wanted or neutral behaviour *Note: if this occurs regularly, <u>also</u> code* **8.4, Habit reversal**	Suggest that the person goes for a walk rather than watches television
8.3	*Habit formation*	Prompt rehearsal and repetition of the behaviour in the same context repeatedly so that the context elicits the behaviour *Note: <u>also</u> code* **8.1, Behavioural practice/rehearsal**	Prompt patients to take their statin tablet before brushing their teeth every evening
8.4	*Habit reversal*	Prompt rehearsal and repetition of an alternative behaviour to **replace** an unwanted habitual behaviour *Note: <u>also</u> code* **8.2, Behaviour substitution**	Ask the person to walk up stairs at work where they previously always took the lift

270

8.5	*Overcorrection*	Ask to repeat the wanted behaviour in an exaggerated way following an unwanted behaviour	Ask to eat only fruit and vegetables the day after a poor diet
8.6	*Generalisation of a target behaviour*	Advise to perform the wanted behaviour, which is already performed in a particular situation, in another situation	Advise to repeat toning exercises learned in the gym when at home
8.7	*Graded tasks*	Set easy-to-perform tasks, making them increasingly difficult, but achievable, until behaviour is performed	Ask the person to walk for 100 yards a day for the first week, then half a mile a day after they have successfully achieved 100 yards, then two miles a day after they have successfully achieved one mile

9. Comparison of outcomes

9.1	*Credible source*	Present verbal or visual communication from a **credible source** in favour of or against the behaviour *Note: code this BCT if source generally agreed on as credible e.g. health professionals, celebrities or words used to indicate expertise or leader in field and if the communication has the aim of persuading; if information about health consequences, <u>also</u> code 5.1, **Information about health consequences**, if about emotional consequences, <u>also</u> code 5.6, **Information about emotional consequences**; if about social, environmental or unspecified consequences <u>also</u> code 5.3, **Information about social and environmental consequences***	Present a speech given by a high status professional to emphasise the importance of not exposing patients to unnecessary radiation by ordering x-rays for back pain

9.2	Pros and cons	Advise the person to identify and compare reasons for wanting (pros) and not wanting to (cons) change the behaviour (includes '**Decisional balance**') Note: if providing information about health consequences, _also_ code 5.1, **Information about health consequences**; if providing information about emotional consequences, _also_ code 5.6, **Information about emotional consequences**; if providing information about social, environmental or unspecified consequences _also_ code 5.3, **Information about social and environmental consequences**	Advise the person to list and compare the advantages and disadvantages of prescribing antibiotics for upper respiratory tract infections
9.3	Comparative imagining of future outcomes	Prompt or advise the imagining and comparing of future outcomes of changed versus unchanged behaviour	Prompt the person to imagine and compare likely or possible outcomes following attending versus not attending a screening appointment
10. Reward and threat			
10.1	Material incentive (behaviour)	Inform that money, vouchers or other valued objects _will be_ delivered if and only if there has been effort and/or progress in performing the behaviour (includes '**Positive reinforcement**') Note: if incentive is social, code 10.5, **Social incentive** if unspecified code 10.6, **Non-specific incentive**, and _not_ 10.1, **Material incentive (behaviour)**; if incentive is for _outcome_, code 10.8, **Incentive (outcome)**. If reward is delivered also code one of: 10.2, **Material reward (behaviour)**; 10.3, **Non-specific reward**; 10.4, **Social reward**, 10.9, **Self-reward**; 10.10, **Reward (outcome)**	Inform that a financial payment will be made each month in pregnancy that the woman has not smoked

| 10.2 | *Material reward (behaviour)* | Arrange for the delivery of money, vouchers or other valued objects if and only if there has been effort and/or progress in performing the behaviour (includes **'Positive reinforcement'**)

*Note: If reward is social, code **10.4**, Social reward, if unspecified code **10.3**, Non-specific reward, and not **10.1**, Material reward (behaviour); if reward is for outcome, code **10.10**, Reward (outcome). If informed of reward in advance of rewarded behaviour, also code one of: **10.1**, Material incentive (behaviour); **10.5**, Social incentive; **10.6**, Non-specific incentive; **10.7**, Self-incentive; **10.8**, Incentive (outcome)* | Arrange for the person to receive money that would have been spent on cigarettes if and only if the smoker has not smoked for one month |
| 10.3 | *Non-specific reward* | Arrange delivery of a reward if and only if there has been effort and/or progress in performing the behaviour (includes **'Positive reinforcement'**)

*Note: if reward is material, code **10.2**, Material reward (behaviour), if social, code **10.4**, Social reward, and not **10.3**, Non-specific reward; if reward is for outcome code **10.10**, Reward (outcome). If informed of reward in advance of rewarded behaviour, also code one of: **10.1**, Material incentive (behaviour); **10.5**, Social incentive; **10.6**, Non-specific incentive; **10.7**, Self-incentive; **10.8**, Incentive (outcome)* | Identify something (e.g. an activity such as a visit to the cinema) that the person values and arrange for this to be delivered if and only if they attend for health screening |

273

10.4	*Social reward*	Arrange verbal or non-verbal reward if and only if there **has been** effort and/or progress in performing the behaviour (includes '**Positive reinforcement**') *Note: if reward is material, code* **10.2, Material reward (behaviour)**, *if unspecified code* **10.3, Non-specific reward**, *and* <u>*not*</u> **10.4, Social reward**; *if reward is for* **outcome** *code* **10.10, Reward (outcome)**. *If informed of reward in advance of rewarded behaviour, also code one of:* **10.1, Material incentive (behaviour); 10.5, Social incentive; 10.6, Non-specific incentive; 10.7, Self-incentive; 10.8, Incentive (outcome)**	Congratulate the person for each day they eat a reduced fat diet
10.5	*Social incentive*	Inform that a verbal or non-verbal reward will be delivered if and only if there has been effort and/or progress in performing the behaviour (includes '**Positive reinforcement**') *Note: if incentive is material, code* **10.1, Material incentive (behaviour)**, *if unspecified code* **10.6, Non-specific incentive**, *and* <u>*not*</u> **10.5, Social incentive**; *if incentive is for* **outcome** *code* **10.8, Incentive (outcome)**. *If reward is delivered also code one of:* **10.2, Material reward (behaviour); 10.3, Non-specific reward; 10.4, Social reward, 10.9, Self-reward; 10.10, Reward (outcome)**	Inform that they will be congratulated for each day they eat a reduced fat diet

10.6	*Non-specific incentive*	Inform that a reward will be delivered if and only if there has been effort and/or progress in performing the behaviour (includes '**Positive reinforcement**') *Note: if incentive is material, code **10.1, Material incentive (behaviour)**, if social, code **10.5, Social incentive** and not **10.6, Non-specific incentive**; if incentive is for **outcome** code **10.8, Incentive (outcome)**. If reward is delivered also code one of: **10.2, Material reward (behaviour); 10.3, Non-specific reward; 10.4, Social reward, 10.9, Self-reward; 10.10, Reward (outcome)***	Identify an activity that the person values and inform them that this will happen if and only if they attend for health screening
10.7	*Self-incentive*	Plan to reward self in future if and only if there has been effort and/or progress in performing the behaviour *Note: if self-reward is material, also code **10.1, Material incentive (behaviour)**, if social, also code **10.5, Social incentive**, if unspecified, also code **10.6, Non-specific incentive**; if incentive is for **outcome** code **10.8, Incentive (outcome)**. If reward is delivered also code one of: **10.2, Material reward (behaviour); 10.3, Non-specific reward; 10.4, Social reward, 10.9, Self-reward; 10.10, Reward (outcome)***	Encourage to provide self with material (e.g. new clothes) or other valued objects if and only if they have adhered to a healthy diet

10.8	Incentive (outcome)	Inform that a reward *will be* delivered if and only if there has been effort and/or progress in achieving the behavioural outcome (*includes '*__Positive reinforcement__*'*) *Note: this includes social, material, self- and non-specific incentives for outcome; if incentive is for the behaviour code 10.5, Social incentive, 10.1, Material incentive (behaviour), 10.6, Non-specific incentive or 10.7, Self-incentive and_not 10.8, Incentive (outcome). If reward is delivered also code one of: 10.2, Material reward (behaviour); 10.3, Non-specific reward; 10.4, Social reward, 10.9, Self-reward; 10.10, Reward (outcome)*	Inform the person that they will receive money if and only if a certain amount of weight is lost
10.9	Self-reward	Prompt self-praise or self-reward if and only if there *has been* effort and/or progress in performing the behaviour *Note: if self-reward is material, also code 10.2, Material reward (behaviour), if social, also code 10.4, Social reward, if unspecified, also code 10.3, Non-specific reward; if reward is for outcome code 10.10, Reward (outcome). If informed of reward in advance of rewarded behaviour, also code one of: 10.1, Material incentive (behaviour); 10.5, Social incentive; 10.6, Non-specific incentive; 10.7, Self-incentive; 10.8, Incentive (outcome)*	Encourage to reward self with material (e.g., new clothes) or other valued objects if and only if they have adhered to a healthy diet

10.10	*Reward (outcome)*	Arrange for the delivery of a reward if and only if there *has been* effort and/or progress in achieving the behavioural **outcome** (includes '<u>**Positive reinforcement**</u>') *Note: this includes social, material, self- and non-specific rewards for outcome; if reward is for the behaviour code 10.4, Social reward, 10.2, Material reward (behaviour), 10.3, Non-specific reward or 10.9, Self-reward and <u>not</u> 10.10, Reward (outcome). If informed of reward in advance of rewarded behaviour, also code one of: 10.1, Material incentive (behaviour); 10.5, Social incentive; 10.6, Non-specific incentive; 10.7, Self-incentive; 10.8, Incentive (outcome)*	Arrange for the person to receive money if and only if a certain amount of weight is lost
10.11	*Future punishment*	Inform that future punishment or removal of reward will be a consequence of performance of an unwanted behaviour (may include fear arousal) (includes '<u>**Threat**</u>')	Inform that continuing to consume 30 units of alcohol per day is likely to result in loss of employment if the person continues
11. Regulation			
11.1	*Pharmacological support*	Provide, or encourage the use of or adherence to, drugs to facilitate behaviour change *Note: if pharmacological support to reduce negative emotions (i.e. anxiety) then <u>also</u> code 11.2, Reduce negative emotions*	Suggest the patient asks the family physician for nicotine replacement therapy to facilitate smoking cessation
11.2	*Reduce negative emotions*	Advise on ways of reducing negative emotions to facilitate performance of the behaviour (includes '<u>**Stress Management**</u>') *Note: if includes analysing the behavioural problem, <u>also</u> code 1.2, Problem solving*	Advise on the use of stress management skills, e.g. to reduce anxiety about joining Alcoholics Anonymous
11.3	*Conserving mental resources*	Advise on ways of minimising demands on mental resources to facilitate behaviour change	Advise to carry food calorie content information to reduce the burden on memory in making food choices

277

11.4	*Paradoxical instructions*	Advise to engage in some form of the unwanted behaviour with the aim of reducing motivation to engage in that behaviour	Advise a smoker to smoke twice as many cigarettes a day as they usually do Tell the person to stay awake as long as possible in order to reduce insomnia

12. Antecedents

12.1	*Restructuring the physical environment*	Change, or advise to change the physical environment in order to facilitate performance of the wanted behaviour or create barriers to the unwanted behaviour (other than prompts/cues, rewards and punishments) *Note: this may also involve 12.3, Avoidance/reducing exposure to cues for the behaviour; if restructuring of the social environment code 12.2, Restructuring the social environment; if only adding objects to the environment, code 12.5, Adding objects to the environment*	Advise to keep biscuits and snacks in a cupboard that is inconvenient to get to Arrange to move vending machine out of the school
12.2	*Restructuring the social environment*	Change, or advise to change the social environment in order to facilitate performance of the wanted behaviour or create barriers to the unwanted behaviour (other than prompts/cues, rewards and punishments) *Note: this may also involve 12.3, Avoidance/reducing exposure to cues for the behaviour; if also restructuring of the physical environment also code 12.1, Restructuring the physical environment*	Advise to minimise time spent with friends who drink heavily to reduce alcohol consumption

12.3	*Avoidance/ reducing exposure to cues for the behaviour*	Advise on how to avoid exposure to specific social and contextual/physical cues for the behaviour, including changing daily or weekly routines *Note: this may also involve 12.1, Restructuring the physical environment and/or 12.2, Restructuring the social environment;* if the BCT includes analysing the behavioural problem, <u>only</u> code *1.2, Problem solving*	Suggest to a person who wants to quit smoking that their social life focus on activities other than pubs and bars which have been associated with smoking
12.4	*Distraction*	Advise or arrange to use an alternative focus for attention to avoid triggers for unwanted behaviour	Suggest to a person who is trying to avoid between-meal snacking to focus on a topic they enjoy (e.g. holiday plans) instead of focusing on food
12.5	*Adding objects to the environment*	Add objects to the environment in order to facilitate performance of the behaviour *Note: Provision of information (e.g. written, verbal, visual) in a booklet or leaflet is insufficient. If this is accompanied by social support, also code 3.2, Social support (practical); if the environment is changed beyond the addition of objects, also code 12.1, Restructuring the physical environment*	Provide free condoms to facilitate safe sex Provide attractive toothbrush to improve tooth brushing technique
12.6	*Body changes*	Alter body structure, functioning or support **directly** to facilitate behaviour change	Prompt strength training, relaxation training or provide assistive aids (e.g. a hearing aid)
13. Identity			
13.1	*Identification of self as role model*	Inform that one's own behaviour may be an example to others	Inform the person that if they eat healthily, that may be a good example for their children

13.2	*Framing/ reframing*	Suggest the deliberate adoption of a perspective or new perspective on behaviour (e.g. its purpose) in order to change cognitions or emotions about performing the behaviour (includes '**Cognitive structuring**'); *If information about consequences then code 5.1, Information about health consequences, 5.6, Information about emotional consequences or 5.3, Information about social and environmental consequences instead of 13.2, Framing/reframing*	Suggest that the person might think of the tasks as reducing sedentary behaviour (rather than increasing activity)
13.3	*Incompatible beliefs*	Draw attention to discrepancies between current or past behaviour and self-image, in order to create discomfort (includes '**Cognitive dissonance**')	Draw attention to a doctor's liberal use of blood transfusion and their self-identification as a proponent of evidence-based medical practice
13.4	*Valued self-identity*	Advise the person to write or complete rating scales about a cherished value or personal strength as a means of affirming the person's identity as part of a behaviour change strategy (includes '**Self-affirmation**')	Advise the person to write about their personal strengths before they receive a message advocating the behaviour change
13.5	*Identity associated with changed behaviour*	Advise the person to construct a new self-identity as someone who 'used to engage with the unwanted behaviour'	Ask the person to articulate their new identity as an 'ex-smoker'
14. Scheduled consequences			
14.1	*Behaviour cost*	Arrange for withdrawal of something valued if and only if an unwanted behaviour is performed (includes '**Response cost**'). *Note if withdrawal of contingent reward code, 14.3, Remove reward*	Subtract money from a prepaid refundable deposit when a cigarette is smoked
14.2	*Punishment*	Arrange for aversive consequence contingent on the performance of the unwanted behaviour	Arrange for the person to wear unattractive clothes following consumption of fatty foods

14.3	*Remove reward*	Arrange for discontinuation of contingent reward following performance of the unwanted behaviour (includes '**Extinction**')	Arrange for the other people in the household to ignore the person every time they eat chocolate (rather than attending to them by criticising or persuading)
14.4	*Reward approximation*	Arrange for reward following any approximation to the target behaviour, gradually rewarding only performance closer to the wanted behaviour (includes '**Shaping**') *Note: also code one of 10.2, Material reward (behaviour); 10.3, Non-specific reward; 10.4, Social reward; 10.9, Self-reward; 10.10, Reward (outcome)*	Arrange reward for any reduction in daily calories, gradually requiring the daily calorie count to become closer to the planned calorie intake
14.5	*Rewarding completion*	Build up behaviour by arranging reward following final component of the behaviour; gradually add the components of the behaviour that occur earlier in the behavioural sequence (includes '**Backward chaining**') *Note: also code one of 10.2, Material reward (behaviour); 10.3, Non-specific reward; 10.4, Social reward, 10.9, Self-reward; 10.10, Reward (outcome)*	Reward eating a supplied low calorie meal; then make reward contingent on cooking and eating the meal; then make reward contingent on purchasing, cooking and eating the meal
14.6	*Situation-specific reward*	Arrange for reward following the behaviour in one situation but not in another (includes '**Discrimination training**') *Note: also code one of 10.2, Material reward (behaviour); 10.3, Non-specific reward; 10.4, Social reward, 10.9, Self-reward; 10.10, Reward (outcome)*	Arrange reward for eating at mealtimes but not between meals

14.7	*Reward incompatible behaviour*	Arrange reward for responding in a manner that is incompatible with a previous response to that situation (includes '**Counter-conditioning**') *Note: also code one of 10.2, Material reward (behaviour); 10.3, Non-specific reward; 10.4, Social reward, 10.9, Self-reward; 10.10, Reward (outcome)*	Arrange reward for ordering a soft drink at the bar rather than an alcoholic beverage
14.8	*Reward alternative behaviour*	Arrange reward for performance of an alternative to the unwanted behaviour (includes '**Differential reinforcement**') *Note: also code one of 10.2, Material reward (behaviour); 10.3, Non-specific reward; 10.4, Social reward, 10.9, Self-reward; 10.10, Reward (outcome); consider also coding 1.2, Problem solving*	Reward for consumption of low fat foods but not consumption of high fat foods
14.9	*Reduce reward frequency*	Arrange for rewards to be made contingent on increasing duration or frequency of the behaviour (includes '**Thinning**') *Note: also code one of 10.2, Material reward (behaviour); 10.3, Non-specific reward; 10.4, Social reward, 10.9, Self-reward; 10.10, Reward (outcome)*	Arrange reward for each day without smoking, then each week, then each month, then every 2 months and so on
14.10	*Remove punishment*	Arrange for removal of an unpleasant consequence contingent on performance of the wanted behaviour (includes '**Negative reinforcement**')	Arrange for someone else to do housecleaning only if the person has adhered to the medication regimen for a week
15. Self-belief			
15.1	*Verbal persuasion about capability*	Tell the person that they can successfully perform the wanted behaviour, arguing against self-doubts and asserting that they can and will succeed	Tell the person that they can successfully increase their physical activity, despite their recent heart attack.
15.2	*Mental rehearsal of successful performance*	Advise to practice imagining performing the behaviour successfully in relevant contexts	Advise to imagine eating and enjoying a salad in a work canteen

15.3	*Focus on past success*	Advise to think about or list previous successes in performing the behaviour (or parts of it)	Advise to describe or list the occasions on which the person had ordered a non-alcoholic drink in a bar
15.4	*Self-talk*	Prompt positive self-talk (aloud or silently) before and during the behaviour	Prompt the person to tell themselves that a walk will be energising

16. Covert learning

16.1	*Imaginary punishment*	Advise to imagine performing the **unwanted** behaviour in a real-life situation followed by imagining an unpleasant consequence (includes '**Covert sensitisation**')	Advise to imagine overeating and then vomiting
16.2	*Imaginary reward*	Advise to imagine performing the **wanted** behaviour in a real-life situation followed by imagining a pleasant consequence (includes '**Covert conditioning**')	Advise the health professional to imagine giving dietary advice followed by the patient losing weight and no longer being diabetic
16.3	*Vicarious consequences*	Prompt observation of the consequences (including rewards and punishments) for others when they perform the behaviour *Note: if observation of health consequences, also code **5.1, Information about health consequences**; if of emotional consequences, also code **5.6, Information about emotional consequences**, if of social, environmental or unspecified consequences, also code **5.3, Information about social and environmental consequences***	Draw attention to the positive comments other staff get when they disinfect their hands regularly

f Following dissemination of BCTTv1 through publication, seminars and workshops, the following changes are anticipated for version 2: The addition of BCT 'Increase positive emotions'. Revised definitions or examples for the following BCTs: 'non-specific reward'; 'information about health consequences'; 'social support'; 'social comparison.
g References to coding relate to using the Taxonomy to describe the content of published interventions.

Appendix 5: Using the BCW, BCTTv1 and TDF to describe an intervention and support implementation: improving compliance with the 'Sepsis Six' care pathway

BCT	Functions	Text description	CAPABILITY				OPPORTUNITY		MOTIVATION					
			Physical	Psychological			Social	Physical	Reflective				Auto	
			S	K	MAD	BR	SI	EN	B Cap	B Con	S/P ID	O	G	EM
Information about health consequences	Education, Persuasion	Staff were told about dangers of Sepsis and effectiveness of following pathway.												▓
Salience of consequences	Persuasion	Staff were told a story of a young patient who had died from Sepsis needlessly.								▓				
Social comparison	Persuasion	Staff were told about high compliance on other wards.							▓		▓			
Demonstration of behaviour	Training	Staff observed & participated in Sepsis Six training simulations.	▓		▓	▓								
Instruction on how to perform the behaviour	Education		▓		▓	▓								
Behavioural practice/ rehearsal Habit formation	Training		▓		▓	▓								
Feedback on behaviour	Persuasion	Staff compliance was monitored by board and intervention implementers and verbal feedback was given in group meetings.					▓			▓	▓			
Adding objects to the environment	Environmental restructure Enablement	Wards were provided with a 'Sepsis Trolley' and 'Sepsis Bags' which contained all instruments required to implement six steps of Sepsis Six.			▓	▓		▓						
Prompts/cues					▓	▓		▓						

285

| | | | CAPABILITY | | | | OPPORTUNITY | | MOTIVATION | | | | | Auto |
| | | | Physical | Psychological | | | Social | Physical | Reflective | | | | | |
BCT	Functions	Text description	S	K	MAD	BR	SI	EN	B Cap	B Con	S/P ID	O	G	EM
Focus on past success	Persuasion	When compliance 'dipped', staff were reminded of past improvements to compliance on their ward.							■					
Adding objects to the environment	Environmental Restructure	Wards were provided with antibiotic cupboards containing all antibiotics likely to be needed for implementation.						■						
Goal setting (behaviour)	Enablement	Staff were given a group target of 95% compliance with all six steps of pathway.				■							■	
Feedback on behaviour	Persuasion	A document detailing real-time compliance was displayed in staff room and updated by intervention facilitators daily.								■				
Self-monitoring (behaviour)	Enablement	Staff filled out and initialled a protocol checklist and sepsis stickers to place in patient notes as they completed each step.				■								
Prompts/cues	Environmental restructure							■						
Problem Solving	Enablement	Staff actively generated solutions to facilitate engagement with Sepsis Six and ensure future compliance in feedback sessions.	■				■							
Instruction on how to perform behaviour	Education	Staff are told about how to identify Sepsis and how and when to implement Sepsis Six and were given this information in written form.												
Goal setting (outcome)	Enablement	Trust set goal of reducing serious untoward incidents related to Sepsis by 50% in pilot wards.				■					■		■	

			CAPABILITY				OPPORTUNITY		MOTIVATION					
			Physical	Psychological			Social	Physical	Reflective					Auto
BCT	Functions	Text description	S	K	MAD	BR	SI	EN	B Cap	B Con	S/P ID	O	G	EM
Discrepancy between current behaviour and goal	Enablement	Variations from the pathway were brought up and compared with 95% goal in staff meetings.											X	
Prompts/cues	Environ mental restructure	Phone app was created to remind staff of triggers and six steps.			X									
Instruction on how to perform behaviour	Education	Phone app instructed how to identify sepsis and carry out Sepsis Six.	X											
Self-monitoring	Enablement	Phone app had timer function whereby staff could monitor when each step was completed.				X								
Adding objects to the environment	Environmental restructure	A Sepsis Six logo was designed and items depicting it were distributed and displayed throughout ward.						X						
Prompts/cues					X									
Feedback on outcome of behaviour	Persuasion	Patients who had been treated with Sepsis Six on the wards were followed-up and their outcomes were feedback to staff weekly.							X			X		X
Verbal persuasion about capability	Persuasion	It was emphasised that Sepsis Six would be easily implemented and become 'second nature'.							X			X		
Feedback on outcome of behaviour	Persuasion	Staff were told about patient outcomes improvements due to their compliance.								X		X		
Instruction on how to perform the behaviour	Education	An antibiotics protocol instructing on how to select appropriate antibiotics for specific patients was added to the pathway protocol.		X										

| BCT | Functions | Text description | CAPABILITY | | | | OPPORTUNITY | | MOTIVATION | | | | | |
| | | | Physical | Psychological | | | Social | Physical | Reflective | | | | | Auto |
			S	K	MAD	BR	SI	EN	B Cap	B Con	S/P ID	O	G	EM
Not specified	Education	Sepsis awareness events were run and publicised throughout trust.												■
Instruction on how to perform the behaviour	Knowledge, Incentivisation	A video that instructed on performing the six steps, included a positive patient story and congratulated staff whom had treated the patient using Sepsis Six was shown.	■	■						■		■		■
Salience of consequences														
Social reward														
Social reward	Incentiv-isation	Staff were given positive reinforcement from the board and intervention facilitators when compliance and patient outcomes improved.							■		■			
Instruction on how to perform the behaviour	Education	A sepsis portal was included on hospital intranet that instructed on how to carry out Sepsis Six.		■										
Social support (unspecified)	Enablement	Staff were encouraged to seek support from superiors & intervention facilitators when there were problems with implementation, e.g. with specific non-compliant staff members.					■							
Social support (unspecified)	Enablement	Staff were supported to feel they had legitimate authority to commence the pathway using their clinical discretion regardless of role.					■				■			

BCT	Functions	Text description	CAPABILITY				OPPORTUNITY		MOTIVATION					
			Physical	Psychological			Social	Physical	Reflective				Auto	
			S	K	MAD	BR	SI	EN	B Cap	B Con	S/P ID	O	G	EM
Feedback on behaviour	Persuasion	Individuals whom were not fully compliant with the pathway were approached after specific incidents and informed about non-compliance. Solutions were generated.												
Problem solving	Enablement													

Appendix 6: Sources referencing the Behaviour Change Wheel

This appendix contains more than 150 peer-review publications, conference presentations, reports, doctoral theses and blogs referencing the Behaviour Change Wheel paper [1]. For an up to date list search 'Behaviour Change Wheel' at www.scholar.google.co.uk.

Amemori, M. (2012). Developing assessment and promotion of tobacco counselling: a cluster-randomised community trial among oral health professionals. Doctoral Thesis, University of Helsinki, http://urn.fi/URN:ISBN:978-952-10-8404-1

Anstey, K. J., Bahar-Fuchs, A., Herath, P., Rebok, G. W., & Cherbuin, N. (2013). A 12-week multidomain intervention versus active control to reduce risk of Alzheimer's disease: study protocol for a randomized controlled trial. Trials, 14. doi: 10.1186/1745-6215-14-60

Atkins, L., & Michie, S. (2013). Changing eating behaviour: What can we learn from behavioural science? Nutrition Bulletin, 38(1), 30-35

Avery, K. N. L., Donovan, J. L., Horwood, J., & Lane, J. A. (2013). Behavior theory for dietary interventions for cancer prevention: a systematic review of utilization and eff ectiveness in creating behavior change. Cancer Causes & Control, 24(3), 409-420. doi: 10.1007/s10552-012-9995-9

Badrick, T. (2012). EBLM in practice. The Clinical Biochemist Reviews, 33(2), 77

Beckmann, M., Parry, A., & Drew, S. (2012). Diagnosing the Gestational Diabetes Mellitus Medical Nutrition Therapy evidence-practice gap: informing. Paper presentaed at the 1st Biennial Australian Implementation Conference, Melbourne, Australia

Belojevic, G. (2013). Internet Based Health Communication: Analysis of Messages on the Websites of Serbian Public Health Institutes. Internet-Based Intelligence in Public Health Emergencies: Early Detection and Response in Disease Outbreak Crises, 97-102. doi: 10.3233/978-1-61499-175-5-97

Bonner, C., Jansen, J., McKinn, S., Irwig, L., Doust, J., Glasziou, P., .. . McCaffery, K. (2013). General practitioners' use of different cardiovascular risk assessment strategies: a qualitative study. Medical Journal of Australia, 199(7), 485-489. doi: 10.5694/ mja13.10133

Borrie, F. R. P. (2013). Interceptive Orthodontics: The Evidence, Current General Dental Practice, and Way Forwards in the UK. Doctoral Thesis, University of Dundee, http://discovery. dundee.ac.uk/portal/files/2011679/Borrie_phd_2013.pdf

Box, D., & Pottas, D. (2013). Improving information security behaviour in the healthcare context. Procedia Technology, 9, 1093-1103

Bradbury, K., Watts, S., Arden-Close, E., Yardley, L., & Lewith, G. (2013). Developing Digital Interventions: A Methodological Guide. Evidence-Based Complementary and Alternative Medicine. Volume 2014, Article ID 561320, 7 pages, http:// dx.doi.org/10.1155/2014/561320

Brake, H.T., Duckers, M. (2013). Early psychosocial interventions after disasters, terrorism and other shocking events: is there a gap between norms and practice in Europe? Eurpoean Journal of Psychotraumatology, 4 10.3402/ejpt.v4i0.19093

Brehaut, J. C., & Eva, K. W. (2012). Building theories of knowledge translation interventions: Use the entire menu of constructs. Implementation Science, 7. doi: 10.1186/1748-5908-7-114

Brennan, N., & Mattick, K. (2013). A systematic review of educational interventions to change behaviour of prescribers in hospital settings, with a particular emphasis on new prescribers. British Journal of Clinical Pharmacology, 75(2), 359-372. doi: 10.1111/j.1365-2125.2012.04397.x

Brown, J., Kotz, D., Michie, S., Stapleton, J., Walmsley, M., & West, R. (2014). How effective and cost-effective was the national mass media smoking cessation campaign 'Stoptober'? Drug and alcohol dependence, 135, 52-58

Brown, K., Beecham, D., & Barrett, H. (2013). The Applicability of Behaviour Change in Intervention Programmes Targeted at Ending Female Genital Mutilation in the EU: Integrating Social Cognitive and Community Level Approaches. Obstetrics and gynecology international, 2013. Volume 2013 (2013), Article ID 324362, 12 pages, http://dx.doi.org/10.1155/2013/324362

Brown, K. E., Bayley, J., & Newby, K. (2013). Serious Game for Relationships and Sex Education: Application of an Intervention Mapping Approach to Development. Serious Games for Healthcare: Applications and Implications, 135-166. doi: 10.4018/978-1-4666-1903-6.ch007

Burke, A. E., Hicks, P. J., & Carraccio, C. (2012). Towards Meaningful Outcomes Assessment: Collaborative Efforts in Pediatric Medical Education. Academic pediatrics, 12(2), 79-80

Burkhart, G. (2013). Is Environment Really A Function? Prevention Science, 1-4. doi: 10.1007/s11121-013-0452-0

Buttriss, J. L. (2013). Food reformulation: the challenges to the food industry. Proceedings of the Nutrition Society, 72(1), 61-69. doi: 10.1017/s0029665112002868

Cane, J., O'Connor, D., & Michie, S. (2012). Validation of the theoretical domains framework for use in behaviour change and implementation research. Implementation Science, 7. doi: 10.1186/1748-5908-7-37

Cattaruzza, M. S., & West, R. (2013). Why do doctors and medical students smoke when they must know how harmful it is? European Journal of Public Health, 23(2), 188-189. doi: 10.1093/eurpub/ckt001

Chaboyer, W., & Gillespie, B. M. (2014). Understanding nurses' views on a pressure ulcer prevention care bundle: a first step towards successful implementation. Journal of clinical nursing. doi: 10.1111/jocn.12587

Chadwick, P., & Benelam, B. (2013). Using behaviour change taxonomies to improve service delivery–A workshop with nutritionists and dietitians. Nutrition Bulletin, 38(1), 108-111

293

Chatterton, T., & Wilson, C. (2014). The 'Four Dimensions of Behaviour' framework: a tool for characterising behaviours to help design better interventions. Transportation Planning and Technology, 37(1), 38-61. doi: 10.1080/03081060.2013.850257

Cole, J. A., Smith, S. M., Hart, N., & Cupples, M. E. (2013). Do practitioners and friends support patients with coronary heart disease in lifestyle change? A qualitative study. BMC Family Practice, 14. doi: 10.1186/1471-2296-14-126

Crowther, C. A., Middleton, P. F., Bain, E., Ashwood, P., Bubner, T., Flenady, V., . . . Team, W. P. (2013). Working to improve survival and health for babies born very preterm: the WISH project protocol. BMC Pregnancy and Childbirth, 13. doi: 10.1186/1471-2393-13-239

Cuffee, Y. L., Hargraves, J. L., Rosal, M., Briesacher, B. A., Schoenthaler, A., Person, S., . . . Allison, J. (2013). Reported racial discrimination, trust in physicians, and medication adherence among inner-city african americans with hypertension. American journal of public health, 103(11), e55-e62

Cullinan, S., Fleming, A., O'Mahony, D., Ryan, C., O'Sullivan, D., Gallagher, P., & Byrne, S. (2013). Why? A qualitative study of potentially inappropriate prescribing in older patients. International Journal of Clinical Pharmacy, 35(6), 1254-1254

Cunningham, S. G. (2013). My Diabetes My Way: an Electronic Personal Health Record for NHS Scotland. Doctoral thesis, University of Dundee. http://discovery.dundee.ac.uk/portal/files/3842503/Cunningham_phd_2014.pdf

Curtis, J., Smith, L., & Jungbluth, L. (2013). Identifying beliefs underlying home composting behaviours in the City of Whitehorse. BehaviourWorks Australia, http://www.behaviourworksaustralia.org/wp-content/uploads/2013/11/Whitehorse-belief-report-Final.pdf

De Vries, R. (2014). Bioethics and Sociology The Wiley Blackwell Encyclopedia of Health, Illness, Behavior, and Society: John Wiley & Sons, Ltd

Desroches, S., Lapointe, A., Ratte, S., Gravel, K., Legare, F., & Tur-cotte, S. (2013). Interventions to enhance adherence to dietary advice for preventing and managing chronic diseases in adults. Cochrane Database of Systematic Reviews(2). doi: 10.1002/14651858.CD008722.pub2

Dizon, J. M., Grimmer-Somers, K., & Kumar, S. (2012). A Qualitative Study on Evidence Based Practice for Filipino Physiother-apists. Open Education Journal, 5. doi: 10.1007/s11121-013-0452-0

Doherty, A., Williamson, W., Hillsdon, M., Hodges, S., Foster, C., & Kelly, P. (2013). Influencing health-related behaviour with wearable cameras: strategies & ethical considerations. Paper presented at the Proceedings of the 4th International Sense-Cam & Pervasive Imaging Conference.

English, M. (2013). Designing a theory-informed, contextually appro-priate intervention strategy to improve delivery of paediatric services in Kenyan hospitals. Implementation Science, 8. doi: 10.1186/1748-5908-8-39

English, M., Gathara, D., Mwinga, S., Ayieko, P., Opondo, C., Alu-vaala, J., . . . Irimu, G. (2014). Adoption of recommended practices and basic technologies in a low-income setting. Archives of Disease in Childhood, archdischild-2013-305561.

Essack, S., Pignatari, A. C., & Global Resp Infection, P. (2013). A framework for the non-antibiotic management of upper re-spiratory tract infections: towards a global change in antibi-otic resistance. International Journal of Clinical Practice, 67, 4-9. doi: 10.1111/ijcp.12335

Fillion, L., de Serres, M., Tremblay, A., Blais, M.-C., Robitaille, M.-A., & Boucher, S. (2014). Sensibiliser les équipes soignantes à la prise en compte de la souffrance psychique: l'expérience du dépistage de la détresse au CHU de Québec. Psycho-Oncolo-gie, 1-8. doi: 10.1007/s11839-014-0456-4

Francis, N. A., Phillips, R., Wood, F., Hood, K., Simpson, S., & Butler, C. C. (2013). Parents' and clinicians' views of an interac-tive booklet about respiratory tract infections in children:

a qualitative process evaluation of the EQUIP randomised controlled trial. BMC Family Practice, 14. doi: 10.1186/1471-2296-14-182

Geelen, D. (2013). Stimulating energy efficiency in households: Comparison of the Livinggreen. eu methods to theory. Livinggreen Scientific Conference – 19 April 2013 – Proceedings, 1-17. http://repository.tudelft.nl/assets/uuid:0cb5b97f-1b34-4301-9e43-1b23cbe975e3/293031.pdf

Gilburt, H., Slade, M., Bird, V., Oduola, S., & Craig, T. K. J. (2013). Promoting recovery-oriented practice in mental health services: a quasi-experimental mixed-methods study. BMC Psychiatry, 13. doi: 10.1186/1471-244x-13-167

Gillespie, B. M., Chaboyer, W., Kang, E., Hewitt, J., Nieuwenhoven, P., & Morley, N. (2014). Postsurgery wound assessment and management practices: a chart audit. Journal of clinical nursing. DOI: 10.1111/jocn.12574

Godin, G. (2012). Le comportement clinique des professionnels de la santé: déterminants d'adoption et méthodes de changement. http://www.chu-sainte-justine.org/documents/General/CdeR/RecheClinique/20120119_GG.pdf

Hanbury, A., Farley, K., Thompson, C., Wilson, P. M., Chambers, D., & Holmes, H. (2013). Immediate versus sustained effects: interrupted time series analysis of a tailored intervention. Implementation Science, 8. doi: 10.1186/1748-5908-8-130

Hansen, I. H., Aachmann, K., Lätheenmäki, L., & Grunert, K. G. (2013). Danskernes forståelse af "de otte kostråd". Retrieved from http://pure.au.dk//portal/files/54487800/ottekostraad.pdf

Harris, J., Williams, T., Hart, O., Hanson, C., Johnstone, G., Muthana, A., & Nield, C. (2014). Using health trainers to promote self-management of chronic pain: can it work? British Journal of Pain, 8(1), 27-33

Hart, T., Tsaousides, T., Zanca, J. M., Whyte, J., Packel, A., Ferraro, M., & Dijkers, M. P. (2014). Toward a Theory-Driven Classification of Rehabilitation Treatments. Archives of Physical Medicine and Rehabilitation, 95(1), S33-S44. doi: 10.1016/j. apmr.2013.05.032

Hendriks, A.-M., Gubbels, J. S., De Vries, N. K., Seidell, J. C., Kremers, S. P., & Jansen, M. W. (2012). Interventions to promote an integrated approach to public health problems: an application to childhood obesity. Journal of Environmental and Public Health, 2012. doi: 10.1155/2012/913236

Hendriks, A.-M., Habraken, J., Jansen, M. W., Gubbels, J. S., De Vries, N. K., van Oers, H., . . . Kremers, S. P. (2014). 'Are we there yet?'–Operationalizing the concept of Integrated Public Health Policies. Health Policy, 114(2), 174-182

Hendriks, A.-M., Jansen, M. W., Gubbels, J. S., De Vries, N. K., Paulussen, T., & Kremers, S. P. (2013). Proposing a conceptual framework for integrated local public health policy, applied to childhood obesity-the behavior change ball. Implementation Science, 8(1), 46. doi:10.1186/1748-5908-8-46

Hendriks, A.-M., Kremers, S. P., Gubbels, J. S., Raat, H., de Vries, N. K., & Jansen, M. W. (2013). Towards health in All policies for childhood obesity prevention. Journal of Obesity, 2013. doi:10.1155/2013/632540

Hill, A. M., Etherton-Beer, C., & Haines, T. P. (2013). Tailored Education for Older Patients to Facilitate Engagement in Falls Prevention Strategies after Hospital Discharge-A Pilot Randomized Controlled Trial. Plos One, 8(5). doi: 10.1371/journal.pone.0063450

Hodgson, S., Namdeo, A., Araujo-Soares, V., & Pless-Mulloli, T. (2012). Towards an interdisciplinary science of transport and health: a case study on school travel. Journal of Transport Geography, 21, 70-79

Hollands, G. J., Shemilt, I., Marteau, T. M., Jebb, S. A., Kelly, M. P., Nakamura, R., . . . Ogilvie, D. (2013). Altering micro-environments to change population health behaviour: towards an evidence base for choice architecture interventions. BMC Public Health, 13. doi: 10.1186/1471-2458-13-1218

Hunt, K., Gray, C. M., Maclean, A., Smillie, S., Bunn, C., & Wyke, S. (2014). Do weight management programmes delivered at professional football clubs attract and engage high risk men? A mixed-methods study. BMC Public Health, 14(1), 50

Hunter, R. F., Davis, M., Tully, M. A., & Kee, F. (2012). The Physical Activity Loyalty Card Scheme: Development and Application of a Novel System for Incentivizing Behaviour Change Electronic Healthcare (pp. 170-177): Springer

Hutchinson, A. (2012). Evidence-based medicine: still not flowing into practice. Prescriber, 23(4), 6-8.

Ilott, I., Gerrish, K., Laker, S., & Bray, K. (2013). Naming and framing the problem: using theories, models and conceptual frameworks Bridging the gap between knowledge and practice. Retrieved from http://clahrc-sy.nihr.ac.uk/images/TK2A/ TK2A%20briefing%20papers/Starter%20for%2010%20No%20 2%20Final%2008-03-2013.pdf.

Jabbour, M., Curran, J., Scott, S. D., Guttman, A., Rotter, T., Ducharme, F. M., . . . Johnson, D. W. (2013). Best strategies to implement clinical pathways in an emergency department setting: study protocol for a cluster randomized controlled trial. Implementation Science, 8. doi: 10.1186/1748-5908-8-55

Jensen, B. B., Lähteenmäki, L., Grunert, K. G., Brown, K. A., Timotijevic, L., Barnett, J., . . . Raats, M. M. (2012). Changing micronutrient intake through (voluntary) behaviour change. The case of folate. Appetite, 58(3), 1014-1022

Johnston, K. N., Young, M., Grimmer, K. A., Antic, R., & Frith, P. A. (2013). Barriers to, and facilitators for, referral to pulmonary rehabilitation in COPD patients from the perspective of Australian general practitioners: a qualitative study. Primary Care Respiratory Journal, 22(3), 319-324. doi: 10.4104/ pcrj.2013.00062

Johnston, M., & Dixon, D. (2013). Developing an integrated biomedical and behavioural theory of functioning and disability: adding models of behaviour to the ICF framework. Health Psychology Review(ahead-of-print), 1-23. doi:10.1080/174371 99.2013.855592

Johnstone, R. P., Jones, A., Fowell, A., Burton, C. R., & Rycroft-Malone, J. (2012). End of life care in Wales: evaluation of a care pathway-based implementation strategy. BMJ Supportive & Palliative Care, 2(2), 150-155

Kalz, M. (2013). Designing self-organized contextualized feedback loops. International Conference on Computer Assisted Assessment (CAA 2013). July, 9-10, 2013, University of Southampton, Southampton, UK. http://caaconference.com.

Kassianos, A. (2013). Understanding Lifestyle-Related Psychosocial Processes After Prostate Cancer Diagnosis. University of Surrey. (Doctoral dissertation). Retrieved from http://epubs. surrey.ac.uk/805144

Kitson, A., Powell, K., Hoon, E., Newbury, J., Wilson, A., & Beilby, J. (2013). Knowledge translation within a population health study: how do you do it? Implementation Science, 8. doi: 10.1186/1748-5908-8-54

Kullgren, J. T., Williams, G. C., & An, L. C. (2013). Patient-centered financial incentives for health: Can employers get change for their dollars? Healthcare, 1(2013) 82-85. http://dx.doi. org/10.1016/j.hjdsi.2013.08.001

Laba, T. L., Bleasel, J., Brien, J. A., Cass, A., Howard, K., Peiris, D., . . . Jan, S. (2013). Strategies to improve adherence to medications for cardiovascular diseases in socioeconomically disadvantaged populations: A systematic review. International Journal of Cardiology, 167(6), 2430-2440. doi: 10.1016/j. ijcard.2013.01.049

Langley, T., Lewis, S., McNeill, A., Gilmore, A., Szatkowski, L., West, R., & Sims, M. (2013). Characterizing tobacco control mass media campaigns in England. Addiction, 108(11), 2001-2008. doi: 10.1111/add.12293

LaRocca, R., Yost, J., Dobbins, M., Ciliska, D., & Butt, M. (2012). The effectiveness of knowledge translation strategies used in public health: a systematic review. BMC Public Health, 12. doi: 10.1186/1471-2458-12-751

Légaré, F., & Zhang, P. (2013). Barriers and facilitators: Strategies for Identification and Measurement Knowledge Translation in Health Care (pp. 121-136): John Wiley & Sons, Ltd.

Légaré, F., Guerrier, M., Nadeau, C., Rheaume, C., Turcotte, S., & Labrecque, M. (2013). Impact of DECISION + 2 on patient and physician assessment of shared decision making implementation in the context of antibiotics use for acute respiratory infections. Implementation Science, 8. doi: 10.1186/1748-5908-8-144

Légaré, F., Politi, M. C., Drolet, R., Desroches, S., Stacey, D., & Bekker, H. (2012). Training health professionals in shared decision-making: An international environmental scan. Patient Education and Counseling, 88(2), 159-169

Légaré, F., Politi, M. C., Drolet, R., Desroches, S., Stacey, D., Bekker, H., & Team, S.-C. (2012). Training health professionals in shared decision-making: An international environmental scan. Patient Education and Counseling, 88(2), 159-169. doi: 10.1016/j.pec.2012.01.002

Lenferink, A., Frith, P., van der Valk, P., Buckman, J., Sladek, R., Cafarella, P., . . . Effing, T. (2013). A self-management approach using self-initiated action plans for symptoms with ongoing nurse support in patients with Chronic Obstructive Pulmonary Disease (COPD) and comorbidities: The COPE-III study protocol. Contemporary Clinical Trials, 36(1), 81-89. doi: 10.1016/j.cct.2013.06.003

Lewis, R.B. (2014).] The Application of Critical Discourse Theory: A Criterion-Referenced Analysis of Reports Relating to Language Revitalisation in Australia and New Zealand. Doctoral Thesis, University of Waikato, http://researchcommons. waikato.ac.nz/bitstream/handle/10289/8585/thesis.pdf?sequence=3

Lockton, D., Harrison, D. J., Cain, R., Stanton, N. A., & Jennings, P. (2013). Exploring Problem-framing through Behavioural Heuristics. International Journal of Design, 7(1), 37-53

Lynagh, M. C., Sanson-Fisher, R. W., & Bonevski, B. (2013). Keeping the 'Goose'on the Menu: Response to Commentaries on Financial Incentives in Health Behaviour Change. International journal of behavioral medicine, 1-4. doi: 10.1007/s12529-013-9342-x

Macleod, M. R., Michie, S., Roberts, I., Dirnagl, U., Chalmers, I., Ioannidis, J. P. A., . . . Glasziou, P. (2014). Biomedical research: increasing value, reducing waste. Lancet, 383(9912), 101-104. doi: 10.1016/s0140-6736(13)62329-6

Marie, N., Luckett, T., Davidson, P. M., Lovell, M., & Lal, S. (2013). Optimal patient education for cancer pain: a systematic review and theory-based meta-analysis. Supportive Care in Cancer, 21(12), 3529-3537. doi: 10.1007/s00520-013-1995-0

McKenzie, J. E., French, S. D., O'Connor, D. A., Mortimer, D. S., Browning, C. J., Russell, G. M., . . . Grp, I. T. (2013). Evidence-based care of older people with suspected cognitive impairment in general practice: protocol for the IRIS cluster randomised trial. Implementation Science, 8. doi: 10.1186/1748-5908-8-91

McKenzie, S. H., & Harris, M. F. (2013). Understanding the relationship between stress, distress and healthy lifestyle behaviour: a qualitative study of patients and general practitioners. BMC Family Practice, 14. doi: 10.1186/1471-2296-14-166

McManus , L. (2013). Tendinopathy: Current Scientific Consensus. Blog, http://physiodevelopment.com/2013/07/tendinopathy-june13/

Michie, S., & Johnston, M. (2012). Theories and techniques of behaviour change: Developing a cumulative science of behaviour change. Health Psychology Review, 6(1), 1-6. doi: 10.1080/17437199.2012.654964

Michie, S., & Johnston, M. (2013). Behavior change techniques Encyclopedia of Behavioral Medicine (pp. 182-187): Springer.

Michie, S., Richardson, M., Johnston, M., Abraham, C., Francis, J., Hardeman, W., . . . Wood, C. E. (2013). The Behavior Change Technique Taxonomy (v1) of 93 Hierarchically Clustered Techniques: Building an International Consensus for the Reporting of Behavior Change Interventions. Annals of Behavioral Medicine, 46(1), 81-95. doi: 10.1007/s12160-013-9486-6

Michie, S., & West, R. (2013). Behaviour change theory and evidence: a presentation to Government. Health Psychology Review, 7(1), 1-22. doi: 10.1080/17437199.2011.649445

Michie, S., West, R., & Spring, B. (2013). Moving From Theory to Practice and Back in Social and Health Psychology. Health Psychology, 32(5), 581-585. doi: 10.1037/a0030205

Mitchell, M. (2011). Considering a new framework for designing public safety'filler'messages on highway variable-message signs: Applying the behaviour change wheel. Journal of the Australasian College of Road Safety, 22(4), 63-72.

Molloy, G. J. (2013). Behavioral Science and Reasons for Nonadherence to Medication. Medical Care, 51(5), 468-468. doi: 10.1097/MLR.0b013e318286e3e9

Molloy, L. E., Moore, J. E., Trail, J., Van Epps, J. J., & Hopfer, S. (2013). Understanding Real-World Implementation Quality and "Active Ingredients" of PBIS. Prevention Science, 14(6), 593-605. doi: 10.1007/s11121-012-0343-9

Moodie, S. T., Kothari, A., Bagatto, M. P., Seewald, R., Miller, L. T., & Scollie, S. D. (2011). Knowledge Translation in Audiology: Promoting the Clinical Application of Best Evidence. Trends in Amplification, 15(1-2), 5-22. doi: 10.1177/1084713811420740

Murphy, A., Szumilas, M., Rowe, D., Landry, K., Martin-Misener, R., Kutcher, S., & Gardner, D. (2014). Pharmacy students' experiences in provision of community pharmacy mental health services. Canadian Pharmacists Journal/Revue des Pharmaciens du Canada, 147(1), 55-65.

Nanjappa, S., & Freeman, R. (2013). Developing an inventory to Assess Parental concerns and Enable child dental Registration (DAPER): Phase 3 Report: Field trial of the PDCS using the CHATTERBOX intervention. Dundee: University of Dundee, Dental Health Services Research Unit. Retrieved from http://discovery.dundee.ac.uk/portal/files/3398837/DAPER_III.pdf.

Newby, K. V., French, D. P., Brown, K. E., & Lecky, D. M. (2013). Increasing young adults' condom use intentions and behaviour through changing chlamydia risk and coping appraisals: study protocol for a cluster randomised controlled trial of efficacy. BMC Public Health, 13. doi: 10.1186/1471-2458-13-528

Nguyen, T. (2011). Acceptance of a pandemic influenza vaccine: a systematic review of surveys of the general public. Infect Drug Resist, 4, 197-207. doi 10.2147/IDR.S23174

Noordman, J., van der Weijden, T., & van Dulmen, S. (2013). Effects of video-feedback on the communication, clinical competence and motivational interviewing skills of practice nurses. Lifestyle counseling by physicians and practice nurses in primary care. doi: 10.1111/jan.12376

Ong, B. N., Morden, A., Brooks, L., Porcheret, M., Edwards, J. J., Sanders, T., . . . Dziedzic, K. (2014). Changing policy and practice: making sense of national guidelines for osteoarthritis. Social Science & Medicine, 106, 101-109. doi:10.1016/j.socscimed.2014.01.036

Ong, B. N., Rogers, A., Kennedy, A., Bower, P., Sanders, T., Morden, A., . . . Stevenson, F. (2014). Behaviour change and social blinkers? The role of sociology in trials of self-management behaviour in chronic conditions. Sociology of health & illness, 36(2), 226-238

Oxford, J., Kozlov, R., & Global Resp Infection, P. (2013). Antibiotic resistance - a call to arms for primary healthcare providers. International Journal of Clinical Practice, 67, 1-3. doi: 10.1111/ijcp.12334

Paul, C. L., Levi, C. R., Catherine, A., Parsons, M. W., Bladin, C. F., Lindley, R. I., . . . Longworth, M. (2014). Thrombolysis ImPlementation in Stroke (TIPS): evaluating the effectiveness of a strategy to increase the adoption of best evidence practice-protocol for a cluster randomised controlled trial in acute stroke care. Implementation Science, 9(1), 38, doi:10.1186/1748-5908-9-38

Peters, G. J. Y., Ruiter, R. A., & Kok, G. (2013). Threatening communication: A qualitative study of fear appeal effectiveness beliefs among intervention developers, policymakers, politicians, scientists, and advertising professionals. International Journal of Psychology. 49(2), 71-79. doi: 10.1002/ijop.12000

Phillips, J.L., Heneka, N., Hickman, L., Lam, L., & Shaw, T. (2014). Impact of a novel online learning module on specialist palliative care nurses' pain assessment competencies and patients' reports of pain: Results from a quasi-experimental pilot study. Palliative Medicine, published online before print March 31, 2014, doi: 10.1177/0269216314527780

Porcheret, M., Main, C., Croft, P., McKinley, R., Hassell, A., & Dziedzic, K. (2014). Development of a behaviour change intervention: a case study on the practical application of theory. Implementation Science, 9, 42, doi:10.1186/1748-5908-9-42

Praveen, D., Patel, A., McMahon, S., Prabhakaran, D., Clifford, G. D., Maulik, P. K., . . . Peiris, D. (2013). A multifaceted strategy using mobile technology to assist rural primary healthcare doctors and frontline health workers in cardiovascular disease risk management: protocol for the SMARTHealth India cluster randomised controlled trial. Implementation Science, 8. doi: 10.1186/1748-5908-8-137

Proctor, E. K., Powell, B. J., Baumann, A. A., Hamilton, A. M., & Santens, R. L. (2012). Writing implementation research grant proposals: ten key ingredients. Implementation Science, 7(1), 96. doi:10.1186/1748-5908-7-96

Proctor, E. K., Powell, B. J., & McMillen, J. C. (2013). Implementation strategies: recommendations for specifying and reporting. Implementation Science, 8(1), 139. doi:10.1186/1748-5908-8-139.

Pruyne, E., Powell, M., & Parsons, J. (2011). Corporate investment in Employee Wellbeing the emerging strategic imperative. https://www.nuffieldhealth.com/sites/default/files/inline/Nuffield-Health-Ashridge-Document.pdf.

Raupach, T., Falk, J., Vangeli, E., Schiekirka, S., Rustler, C., Grassi, M. C., . . . West, R. (2012). Structured smoking cessation training for health professionals on cardiology wards: a prospective study. European journal of preventive cardiology, 1-8. doi: 10.1177/2047487312462803.

Reid, W. D., & Hoens, A. (2012). Clinicians' Commentary on You et al. 1. Physiotherapy Canada, 64(2), 176-177

Richards, D. (2013). Improving outcomes–changing behaviours. Evidence-based dentistry, 14(4), 98-98

Riis, A., Jensen, C. E., Bro, F., Maindal, H. T., Petersen, K. D., & Jensen, M. B. (2013). Enhanced implementation of low back pain guidelines in general practice: study protocol of a cluster randomised controlled trial. Implementation Science, 8. doi: 10.1186/1748-5908-8-124

Robinson, E., Aveyard, P., Daley, A., Jolly, K., Lewis, A., Lycett, D., & Higgs, S. (2013). Eating attentively: a systematic review and meta-analysis of the effect of food intake memory and awareness on eating. American Journal of Clinical Nutrition, 97(4), 728-742. doi: 10.3945/ajcn.112.045245

Robinson, E., Higgs, S., Daley, A. J., Jolly, K., Lycett, D., Lewis, A., & Aveyard, P. (2013). Development and feasibility testing of a smart phone based attentive eating intervention. BMC Public Health, 13. doi: 10.1186/1471-2458-13-639

Rohrbasser, A., Mickan, S., & Harris, J. (2013). Exploring why quality circles work in primary health care: a realist review protocol. Systematic reviews, 2(1), 110. doi:10.1186/2046-4053-2-110.

Rubin, S. E., Davis, K., & McKee, M. D. (2013). New York City physicians' views of providing long-acting reversible contraception to adolescents. The Annals of Family Medicine, 11(2), 130-136

Rutten, G. M., Harting, J., Bartholomew, L. K., Braspenning, J. C., van Dolder, R., Heijmans, M. F., . . . Rutten, S. T. (2014). Development of a theory-and evidence-based intervention to enhance implementation of physical therapy guidelines for the management of low back pain. Archives of Public Health, 72(1), 1. doi: 10.1186/2049-3258-72-1

Rycroft-Malone, J., Seers, K., Chandler, J., Hawkes, C. A., Crichton, N., Allen, C., . . . Strunin, L. (2013). The role of evidence, context, and facilitation in an implementation trial: implications for the development of the PARIHS framework. Implementation Science, 8. doi: 10.1186/1748-5908-8-28

Sanson-Fisher, R. W., D'Este, C. A., Carey, M. L., Noble, N., & Paul, C. L. (2014). Evaluation of Systems-Oriented Public Health Interventions: Alternative Research Designs. Annual review of public health. 35, 9-27. doi: 10.1146/annurev-publhealth-032013-182445

Scott, A., Docking, S., Vicenzino, B., Alfredson, H., Zwerver, J., Lundgreen, K., . . . Danielson, P. (2013). Sports and exercise-related tendinopathies: a review of selected topical issues by participants of the second International Scientific Tendinopathy Symposium (ISTS) Vancouver 2012. British Journal of Sports Medicine, 47(9), 536-544. doi: 10.1136/bjsports-2013-092329

Scott, S. D., Albrecht, L., O'Leary, K., Ball, G. D., Hartling, L., Hofmeyer, A., . . . Newton, A. S. (2012). Systematic review of knowledge translation strategies in the allied health professions. Implement Sci, 7(1), 70-70

Sørensen, K., & Brand, H. (2011). Health literacy—A strategic asset for corporate social responsibility in Europe. Journal of health communication, 16(sup3), 322-327

Spotswood, F., French, J., Tapp, A., & Stead, M. (2012). Some reasonable but uncomfortable questions about social marketing. Journal of Social Marketing, 2(3), 163-175

Spruijt-Metz, D., O'Reilly, G. A., Cook, L., Page, K. A., & Quinn, C. (2014). Behavioral Contributions to the Pathogenesis of Type 2 Diabetes. Current diabetes reports, 14(4), 1-10

Storr, J., Wigglesworth, N., & Kilpatrick, C. (2013). Integrating human factors with infection prevention and control. The Health Foundation. http://www.health.org.uk/public/ cms/75/76/313/4248/Integrating%20human%20factors%20 with%20infection%20prevention%20and%20control.pdf?re-alName=Hyoy8o.pdf

Strong, S. (2013). Laying the foundation for self-management support in a recovery framework. (Doctoral dissertation). Open Access Dissertations and Theses. Paper 8152. Retrieved from http://digitalcommons.mcmaster.ca/opendissertations/8152.

Tapp, A., & Spotswood, F. (2013). From the 4Ps to COM-SM: reconfiguring the social marketing mix. Journal of Social Marketing, 3(3), 206-222

Taylor, G., & van Havill, M. (2013). Facebook vs MySpaceHealthInformation: Why Patient Engagement Hasn't Left the Starting Gates. Paper presented at the New Zealand Health Informatics Conference, Rotorua, New Zealand. . Retrieved from http://www.hinz.org.nz/uploads/file/2013conference/Facebook%20vs%20MySpaceHealthInformation%20-%20Taylor. pdf

Te Brake, H., & Dückers, M. (2012). Early psychosocial interventions after disasters, terrorism and other shocking events: is there a gap between norms and practice in Europe? European Journal of Psychotraumatology, 4.

Van den Branden, S., Van den Broucke, S., Leroy, R., Declerck, D., Bogaerts, K., & Hoppenbrouwers, K. (2013). Effect evaluation of an oral health promotion intervention in preschool children. The European Journal of Public Health. doi: 1-6.10.1093/eurpub/ckt204

van der Wees, P. J., Zagers, C. A. M., de Die, S. E., Hendriks, E. J. M., Nijhuis-van der Sanden, M. W. G., & de Bie, R. A. (2013). Developing a questionnaire to identify perceived barriers for implementing the Dutch physical therapy COPD clinical practice guideline. BMC Health Services Research, 13. doi: 10.1186/1472-6963-13-159

van Koperen, M. T., van der Kleij, R. M., Renders, C. C., Crone, M. M., Hendriks, A.-M. A., Jansen, M. M., . . . Molleman, G. G. (2014). Design of CIAO, a research program to support the development of an integrated approach to prevent over-weight and obesity in the Netherlands. BMC Obesity, 1(5), 1-12. doi:10.1186/2052-9538-1-5

Vidotto, G., Bertolotti, G., Zotti, A., Marchi, S., & Tavazzi, L. (2013). Cognitive and Emotional Factors Affecting Avoidable De-cision-Making Delay in Acute Myocardial Infarction Male Adults. International Journal of Medical Sciences, 10(9), 1174-1180. doi: 10.7150/ijms.5800

Voils, C. I., Chang, Y., Crandell, J., Leeman, J., Sandelowski, M., & Maciejewski, M. L. (2012). Informing the dosing of interven-tions in randomized trials. Contemporary Clinical Trials, 33(6), 1225-1230

Ward, D. S., Vaughn, A., & Story, M. (2013). Expert and stakeholder consensus on priorities for obesity prevention research in early care and education settings. Childhood Obesity, 9(2), 116-124

Watson, R., & Wyness, L. (2013). 'Don't tell me what to eat!'–Ways to engage the population in positive behaviour change. Nutri-tion Bulletin, 38(1), 23-29

Watt, R. G., Draper, A. K., Ohly, H. R., Rees, G., Pikhart, H., Cooke, L., . . . McGlone, P. (2013). Methodological development of an exploratory randomised controlled trial of an early years' nutrition intervention: the CHERRY programme (Choosing Healthy Eating when Really Young). Maternal & Child Nu-trition. , 10(2), 280-294. doi: 10.1111/mcn.12061

Wein, T. (2012). The Perfect and the Possible: Seeking a Frugal Model of Behaviour Change. Retrieved from http://www.bdinstitute.org/wp-content/uploads/2012/10/PerfectPossible.pdf

Wells, V., Wyness, L., & Coe, S. (2013). The British Nutrition Foundation's 45th Anniversary Conference: Behaviour change in relation to healthier lifestyles. Nutrition Bulletin, 38(1), 100-107

Wensing, M., Bosch, M., & Grol, R. (2013). Developing and selecting knowledge translation interventions Knowledge Translation in Health Care (pp. 150-162): John Wiley & Sons, Ltd.

West, R. (2011). Preventing tobacco companies from advertising using their packaging could be an important component of comprehensive tobacco control: A commentary on Australia's plain packaging of cigarettes. Drug and Alcohol Review, 30(6), 681-682. doi: 10.1111/j.1465-3362.2011.00369.x

West, R., & Brown, J. (2013). A synthetic theory of motivation Theory of Addiction, Second Edition (pp. 192-228): Wiley-Blackwell

Wilkinson, S. A., McCray, S., Beckmann, M., Parry, A., & McIntyre, H. D. (2014). Barriers and enablers to translating gestational diabetes guidelines into practice. Practical Diabetes, 31(2), 67-72a

Wilkinson, S. A., Poad, D., & Stapleton, H. (2013). Maternal overweight and obesity: a survey of clinicians' characteristics and attitudes, and their responses to their pregnant clients. BMC Pregnancy and Childbirth, 13(117), 1-8. doi:10.1186/1471-2393-13-117

Wilkinson, S. A., & Stapleton, H. (2012). Overweight and obesity in pregnancy: The evidence-practice gap in staff knowledge, attitudes and practices. Australian & New Zealand Journal of Obstetrics & Gynaecology, 52(6), 588-592. doi: 10.1111/ajo.12011

Willamowski, J. K., Hoppenot, Y., & Grasso, A. (2013). Promoting sustainable print behavior. Paper presented at the CHI'13 Extended Abstracts on Human Factors in Computing Systems. Paper presented at the CHI'13 Extended Abstracts on Human Factors in Computing Systems in Paris, France. BMC Pregnancy and Childbirth, 13, 117 doi:10.1186/1471-2393-13-117

Willis, N., Hill, S., Kaufman, J., Lewin, S., Kis-Rigo, J., Freire, S. B. D., . . . Wiysonge, C. S. (2013). "Communicate to vaccinate": the development of a taxonomy of communication interventions to improve routine childhood vaccination. BMC International Health and Human Rights, 13. doi: 10.1186/1472-698x-13-23

Wills, J., Crichton, N., Lorenc, A., & Kelly, M. (2014). Using population segmentation to inform local obesity strategy in England. Health promotion international, 1-9. doi:10.1093/heapro/dau004

Wilson, L. M., Avila Tang, E., Chander, G., Hutton, H. E., Odelola, O. A., Elf, J. L., . . . Haberl, E. B. (2012). Impact of tobacco control interventions on smoking initiation, cessation, and prevalence: a systematic review. Journal of environmental and public health, 2012, 1-36. doi:10.1155/2012/961724.

Woodside, J. V., Young, I. S., & McKinley, M. C. (2013). Fruits and vegetables: measuring intake and encouraging increased consumption. Proceedings of the Nutrition Society, 72(2), 236-245. doi: 10.1017/s0029665112003059

Young, T., Rohwer, A., Volmink, J., & Clarke, M. (2014). What Are the Effects of Teaching Evidence-Based Health Care (EBHC)? Overview of Systematic Reviews. Plos One, 9(1) doi:10.1371/journal.pone.0086706.

Zardo, P., Collie, A., & Livingstone, C. (2014). External factors affecting decision-making and use of evidence in an Australian public health policy environment. Social Science & Medicine, 108, 120-127.

Zhuang, X., & Wu, C. (2013). Saving Energy when using Air conditioners in Offices—Behavioral Pattern and Design Indications. Energy and Buildings. In press. http://dx.doi.org/10.1016/j.enbuild.2013.11.042

References

1. Michie S, van Stralen M, West R. The behaviour change wheel: A new method for characterising and designing behaviour change interventions. Implementation Science. 2011;6:42.

2. Michie S, Richardson M, Johnston M, Abraham C, Francis J, Hardeman W, et al. The behavior change technique taxonomy (v1) of 93 hierarchically clustered techniques: building an international consensus for the reporting of behavior change interventions. Annals of Behavioral Medicine. 2013;46(1):81-95.

3. Abraham C, Michie S. A taxonomy of behavior change techniques used in interventions. Health Psychology. 2008;27(3):379-87.

4. Leeman J, Baernholdt M, Sandelowski M. Developing a theory-based taxonomy of methods for implementing change in practice. Journal of Advanced Nursing. 2007;58(2):191-200.

5. Lowe D, Ryan R, Santesso N, Hill S. Development of a taxonomy of interventions to organise the evidence on consumers medicines use. Patient Education and Counseling. 2011;85(2):e101-e7.

6. Michie S, Ashford S, Sniehotta FF, Dombrowski SU, Bishop A, French DP. A refined taxonomy of behaviour change techniques to help people change their physical activity and healthy eating behaviours: The CALO-RE taxonomy. Psychology & Health. 2011;26(11):1479-98.

7. Michie S, Hyder N, Walia A, West R. Development of a taxonomy of behaviour change techniques used in individual behavioural support for smoking cessation. Addictive Behaviors. 2011;36(4):315-9.

8. Abraham C, Good A, Huedo-Medina TB, Warren MR, Johnson BT. Reliability and Utility of the SHARP Taxonomy

of Behaviour Change Techniques. Psychology & Health. 2012;27(Suppl 1):1-2.

9. Michie S, Whittington C, Hamoudi Z, Zarnani F, Tober G, West R. Identification of behaviour change techniques to reduce excessive alcohol consumption. Addiction. 2012;107(8):1431-40.

10. Cane J, O'Connor D, Michie S. Validation of the theoretical domains framework for use in behaviour change and implementation research. Implementation Science. 2012;7:37.

11. Craig P, Dieppe P, Macintyre S, Michie S, Nazareth I, Petticrew M. Developing and evaluating complex interventions: the new Medical Research Council guidance. BMJ. 2008;337:a1655.

12. Michie S, Campbell R, Brown J, West R. ABC of Behaviour Change Theories. London: Silverback Publishing; 2014.

13. Institute for Government. MINDSPACE: Influencing Behaviour Through Public Policy. Institute for Government, the Cabinet Office; 2010.

14. Bartholomew L, Parcel G, Kok G, Gottlieb N, Fernandez M. Planning Health Promotion Programmes: An Intervention Mapping Approach. 3rd ed: Jossey Bass; 2011.

15. Taggar J, Coleman T, Lewis S, Szatkowski L. The impact of the Quality and Outcomes Framework (QOF) on the recording of smoking targets in primary care medical records: cross-sectional analyses from The Health Improvement Network (THIN) database. BMC Public Health. 2012;12:329.

16. Jackson C, Eliasson L, Barber N, Weinman J. Applying COM-B to medication adherence: A suggested framework for research and interventions The European Health Psychologist. 2014;16(1):7-17.

17. Nuffield Council on Bioethics. Public health: ethical issues. Cambridge Publishers Ltd; 2007.

18. Michie S, Johnston M. Changing clinical behaviour by making guidelines specific. BMJ. 2004;328(7435):343-5.

19. Steinmo S, Fuller C, Stone S, Michie S. Using a behavioural theory framework to design an intervention to improve implementation of the "Sepsis Six" at the Royal Free. In preparation.

20. West R, Brown J. Theory of Addiction. 2nd ed: John Wiley & Sons Ltd; 2013.

21. West SL, O'Neal KK. Project D.A.R.E. Outcome Effectiveness Revisited. American Journal of Public Health. 2004;94(6):1027-9.

22. Babor TF. Alcohol: No Ordinary Commodity: Research and Public Policy. 2nd ed: Oxford University Press; 2010.

23. Rubin GJ, Potts HW, Michie S. The impact of communications about swine flu (influenza A H1N1v) on public responses to the outbreak: results from 36 national telephone surveys in the UK. Health Technology Assessment. 2010;14(34):183-266.

24. Bonner C, Jansen J, McKinn S, Irwig L, Doust J, Glasziou P, et al. General practitioners' use of different cardiovascular risk assessment strategies: a qualitative study. Medical Journal of Australia. 2013;199(7):485-9.

25. Wildman M, Arden M, Curley R, Hoo Z, Michie S. A conceptual framework to develop and understand adherence interventions in Cystic Fibrosis. In preparation

26. Curtis K. Development of a theoretically grounded paediatric weight management app. In preparation

27. Robinson E, Higgs S, Daley A, Jolly K, Lycett D, Lewis A, et al. Development and feasibility testing of a smart phone based attentive eating intervention. BMC Public Health. 2013;13:639.

28. Sallis A. COM-B analysis of GP fit note behaviour (internal document). 2013.

29. Michie S, Johnston M, Abraham C, Lawton R, Parker D, Walker A, et al. Making psychological theory useful for implementing evidence based practice: a consensus approach. Quality & Safety in Health Care. 2005;14(1):26-33.

30. Davis R, Campbell R, Hilden Z, Hobbs L, Michie. Theories of behaviour and behaviour change across the social and behavioural sciences: a scoping review. Under review. 2014

31. Borrelli B. The Assessment, Monitoring, and Enhancement of Treatment Fidelity In Public Health Clinical Trials. Journal of Public Health Dentistry. 2011;71(Suppl 1):S52-S63.

32. Glanz K, Bishop DB. The role of behavioral science theory in development and implementation of public health interventions. Annual Review of Public Health. 2010;31:399-418.

33. Noar SM, Benac CN, Harris MS. Does tailoring matter? Meta-analytic review of tailored print health behavior change interventions. Psychological Bulletin. 2007;133(4):673-93.

34. Noar SM, Zimmerman RS. Health Behavior Theory and cumulative knowledge regarding health behaviors: are we moving in the right direction? Health Education Research. 2005;20(3):275-90.

35. Trifiletti LB, Gielen AC, Sleet DA, Hopkins K. Behavioral and social sciences theories and models: are they used in unintentional injury prevention research? Health Education Research. 2005;20(3):298-307.

36. Webb TL, Sniehotta FF, Michie S. Using theories of behaviour change to inform interventions for addictive behaviours. Addiction. 2010;105(11):1879-92.

37. Prestwich A, Sniehotta FF, Whittington C, Dombrowski SU, Rogers L, Michie S. Does Theory Influence the Effectiveness of Health Behavior Interventions? Meta-Analysis. Health Psychology. 2013;Epub ahead of print.

38. Taylor N, Parveen S, Robins V, Slater B, Lawton R. Development and initial validation of the Influences on Patient Safety Behaviours Questionnaire. Implementation Science. 2013;8:81.

39. Taylor N, Lawton R, Conner M. Development and initial validation of the determinants of physical activity questionnaire. International Journal of Behavioral Nutrition and Physical Activity. 2013;10:74.

40. Huijg J, Gebhardt W, Crone M, Dusseldorp E, Presseau J. Discriminant content validity of a theoretical domains framework questionnaire for use in implementation research. Implementation Science. 2014;9:11.

41. Francis JJ, O'Connor D, Curran J. Theories of behaviour change synthesised into a set of theoretical groupings: introducing a thematic series on the theoretical domains framework. Implementation Science. 2012;7:35.

42. Beenstock J, Sniehotta FF, White M, Bell R, Milne EM, Araujo-Soares V. What helps and hinders midwives in engaging with pregnant women about stopping smoking? A cross-sectional survey of perceived implementation difficulties among midwives in the North East of England. Implementation Science. 2012;7:36.

43. Amemori M, Michie S, Korhonen T, Murtomaa H, Kinnunen T. Assessing implementation difficulties in tobacco use prevention and cessation counselling among dental providers. Implementation Science. 2011;6:50.

44. French S, Green S, O'Connor D, McKenzie J, Francis J, Michie S, et al. Developing theory-informed behaviour change interventions to implement evidence into practice: a systematic approach using the Theoretical Domains Framework. Implementation Science. 2012;7:38.

45. Francis J, Tinmouth A, Stanworth S, Grimshaw J, Johnston M, Hyde C, et al. Using theories of behaviour to understand transfusion prescribing in three clinical contexts in two countries: Development work for an implementation trial. Implementation Science. 2009;4:70.

46. Dyson J, Lawton R, Jackson C, Cheater F. Does the use of a theoretical approach tell us more about hand hygiene behaviour? The barriers and levers to hand hygiene. Journal of Infection Prevention. 2011;12(1):17-24.

47. Michie S, Pilling S, Garety P, Whitty P, Eccles M, Johnston M, et al. Difficulties implementing a mental health guideline: an exploratory investigation using psychological theory. Implementation Science. 2007;2:8.

48. Treweek S, Ricketts IW, Francis J, Eccles M, Bonetti D, Pitts NB, et al. Developing and evaluating interventions to reduce inappropriate prescribing by general practitioners of antibiotics for upper respiratory tract infections: A randomised controlled trial to compare paper-based and web-based modelling experiments. Implementation Science. 2011;6:16.

49. Michie S, Johnston M, Francis J, Hardeman W, Eccles M. From Theory to Intervention: Mapping Theoretically Derived Behavioural Determinants to Behaviour Change Techniques. Applied Psychology. 2008;57(4):660-80.

50. Atkins L, Hunkeler E, Jensen C, Michie S, Corley D. Identifying factors influencing variation in physician adenoma detection rates for screening colonoscopy exams: A focus group study using the COM-B model and Theoretical Domains Framework. In preparation

51. Atkins L, Burton A, Walters K, Gray B, Michie S, Osborn D. Developing a theory-based intervention to reduce cardiovascular disease risk in people with severe mental illness: Findings from a systematic review and focus group study UK Society for Behavioural Medicine; Oxford, UK2013.

52. Rubin SE, Davis K, McKee MD. New York City Physicians' Views of Providing Long-Acting Reversible Contraception to Adolescents. Annals of Family Medicine. 2013;11(2):130-6.

53. Atkins L, Sheals K, Jackson R, Michie S. Evaluating a waste management intervention to promote recycling. In preparation

54. Stead LF, Bergson G, Lancaster T. Physician advice for smoking cessation. Cochrane Database of Systematic Reviews. 2008(2):CD000165.

55. Aveyard P, West R. Managing smoking cessation. BMJ. 2007;335(7609):37-41.

56. Abraham C, Kelly MP, West R, Michie S. The UK National Institute for Health and Clinical Excellence public health guidance on behaviour change: A brief introduction. Psychology, Health & Medicine. 2008;14(1):1-8.

57. Jebb S. Portion size and obesity: emerging research and implications for policy and practice. Keynote speech. UKSBM Conference 2013. Oxford.

58. Senn H, Wilton J, Sharma M, Fowler S, Tan DH. Knowledge of and opinions on HIV preexposure prophylaxis among front-line service providers at Canadian AIDS service organizations. AIDS Research and Human Retroviruses. 2013;29(9):1183-9.

59. Wheelock A, Eisingerich AB, Gomez GB, Gray E, Dybul MR, Piot P. Views of policymakers, healthcare workers and NGOs on HIV pre-exposure prophylaxis (PrEP): a multinational qualitative study. BMJ Open. 2012;2:e001234.

60. Tripathi A, Ogbuanu C, Monger M, Gibson JJ, Duffus WA. Preexposure Prophylaxis for HIV Infection: Healthcare Providers' Knowledge, Perception, and Willingness to Adopt Future Implementation in the Southern US. Southern Medical Journal. 2012;105(4):199-206.

61. White JM, Mimiaga MJ, Krakower DS, Mayer KH. Evolution of Massachusetts physician attitudes, knowledge, and experience regarding the use of antiretrovirals for HIV prevention. AIDS Patient Care and STDs. 2012;26(7):395-405.

62. Arnold EA, Hazelton P, Lane T, Christopoulos KA, Galindo GR, Steward WT, et al. A Qualitative Study of Provider Thoughts on Implementing Pre-Exposure Prophylaxis (PrEP) in Clinical Settings to Prevent HIV Infection. PloS ONE. 2012;7(7):e40603.

63. Puro V, Palummieri A, De Carli G, Piselli P, Ippolito G. Attitude towards antiretroviral pre-exposure prophylaxis (PrEP) prescription among HIV specialists. BMC Infectious Diseases. 2013;13:217.

64. Dahlgren G, Whitehead M. Tackling inequalities in health: what can we learn from what has been tried? Working paper prepared for the King's Fund International Seminar on Tackling Inequalities in Health. 1993. In: European strategies for tackling social inequities in health: Levelling up Part 2 [Internet]. Copenhagen: WHO Regional office for Europe: http://www.euro.who.int/__data/assets/pdf_file/0018/103824/E89384.pdf. 2007.

65. English M. Designing a theory-informed, contextually appropriate intervention strategy to improve delivery of paediatric services in Kenyan hospitals. Implementation Science. 2013;8:39.

66. Hanbury A, Farley K, Thompson C, Wilson P, Chambers D, Holmes H. Immediate versus sustained effects: interrupted time series analysis of a tailored intervention. Implementation Science. 2013;8:130.

67. Department of Health. A Smoke-free Future: A Comprehensive Tobacco Control Strategy for England. 2010.

68. National Institute for Health and Clinical Excellence. Obesity: the prevention, identification, assessment and management of overweight and obesity in adults and children. 2006.

69. Michie S, Johnston M. Behavior Change Techniques. In: Gellman M, Turner JR, editors. Encyclopedia of Behavioral Medicine. New York: Springer; 2013. p. 182-7.

70. West R, Walia A, Hyder N, Shahab L, Michie S. Behavior change techniques used by the English Stop Smoking Services and their associations with short-term quit outcomes. Nicotine & Tobacco Research. 2010;12(7):742-7.

71. National Institute for Health and Care Excellence. Behaviour Change at Population, Community and Individual Levels [NICE Public Health Guidance 6]. London: National Institute for Health and Care Excellence; 2007.

72. Abraham C, Johnston M, Wood C, Francis J, Hardeman W, Richardson M, et al. Testing the identification of behavior change techniques (BCTs) defined by the "BCT Taxonomy version 1" (BCTTv1) in intervention descriptions. In preparation

73. Cane J, Richardson M, Johnston M, Lahda R, Michie S. From lists of behaviour change techniques (BCTs) to structured hierarchies: comparison of two methods of developing a hierarchy of BCTs. British Journal of Health Psychology. In press.

74. Fuller C, Michie S, Savage J, McAteer J, Besser S, Charlett A, et al. The Feedback Intervention Trial (FIT) — Improving Hand-Hygiene Compliance in UK Healthcare Workers: A Stepped Wedge Cluster Randomised Controlled Trial. PLoS ONE. 2012;7(10):e41617.

75. Lancaster T, Stead LF. Individual behavioural counselling for smoking cessation. Cochrane Database of Systematic Reviews. 2005(2):CD001292.

76. Michie S, Churchill S, West R. Identifying Evidence-Based Competences Required to Deliver Behavioural Support for Smoking Cessation. Annals of Behavioral Medicine. 2011;41(1):59-70.

77. Araujo-Soares V, McIntyre T, MacLennan G, Sniehotta FF. Development and exploratory cluster-randomised opportunistic trial of a theory-based intervention to enhance physical activity among adolescents. Psychology & Health. 2009;24(7):805-22.

78. McKenzie JE, French SD, O'Connor DA, Mortimer DS, Browning CJ, Russell GM, et al. Evidence-based care of older people with suspected cognitive impairment in general practice: protocol for the IRIS cluster randomised trial. Implementation Science. 2013;8:91.

79. Murphy K, O'Connor DA, Browning CJ, French SD, Michie S, Francis JJ, et al. Understanding diagnosis and management of dementia and guideline implementation in general practice: A qualitative study using the Theoretical Domains Framework. . Implementation Science. 2014;9:31.

80. Porcheret M, Main C, Croft P, McKinley R, Hassell A, Dziedzic K. Development of a behaviour change intervention: a case study on the practical application of theory. Implementation Science. 2014;9:42, DOI: 10.1186/1748-5908-9-42

81. Grol R, Wensing M, Eccles M. Improving Patient Care - The Implementation of Change in Clinical Practice. London: Elsevier; 2004.

82. Davidson KW, Goldstein M, Kaplan RM, Kaufmann PG, Knatterud GL, Orleans CT, et al. Evidence-based behavioral

medicine: what is it and how do we achieve it? Annals of Behavioral Medicine. 2003;26(3):161-71.

83. Stead LF, Lancaster T. Group behaviour therapy programmes for smoking cessation. Cochrane Database of Systematic Reviews. 2002(3):CD001007.

84. Durkin S, Wakefield M. Comparative responses to radio and television anti-smoking advertisements to encourage smoking cessation. Health Promotion International. 2010;25(1):5-13.

85. Ryder J, Davies L, Bibby J. P128 Smoking cessation educational poster campaign. Thorax. 2011;66(Suppl 4):A119.

86. Bala M, Strzeszynski L, Cahill K. Mass media interventions for smoking cessation in adults. Cochrane Database of Systematic Reviews. 2008(1):CD004704.

87. Hall S, Bishop AJ, Marteau TM. Increasing readiness to stop smoking in women undergoing cervical screening: evaluation of two leaflets. Nicotine & Tobacco Research. 2003;5(6):821-6.

88. Michie S, Brown J, Geraghty A, Miller S, Yardley L, Gardner B, et al. Development of StopAdvisor: A theory-based interactive internet-based smoking cessation intervention. Translational Behavioral Medicine: Practice, Policy and Research. 2012;2(3):263-75.

89. Kaur H, Wai Chi W, Michie S, Kotz D, West R. Preliminary evaluation of SmokeFree 28 (SF28) - a smartphone application to aid smoking cessation. In preparation

90. Stead LF, Perera R, Lancaster T. Telephone counselling for smoking cessation. Cochrane Database of Systematic Reviews. 2006(3):CD002850.

91. Free C, Knight R, Robertson S, Whittaker R, Edwards P, Zhou W, et al. Smoking cessation support delivered via mobile phone text messaging (txt2stop): a single-blind, randomised trial. The Lancet. 2011;378(9785):49-55.

92. Riley W, Jerome A, Behar A, Weil J. Computer and manual self-help behavioral strategies for smoking reduction: initial feasibility and one-year follow-up. Nicotine & Tobacco Research. 2002;4(Suppl 2):S183-S8.

93. Dombrowski S, Sniehotta F, Avenell A, Johnston M, MacLennan G, Araujo-Soares V. Identifying active ingredients in complex behavioural interventions for obese adults with obesity-related comorbidities or additional risk factors for co-morbidities: a systematic review. Health Psychology Review. 2012;6(1):7-32.

94. Lorencatto F, West R, Stavri Z, Michie S. How Well Is Intervention Content Described in Published Reports of Smoking Cessation Interventions? Nicotine & Tobacco Research. 2013;15(7):1273-82.

95. Lorencatto F, West R, Seymour N, Michie S. Developing a method for specifying the components of behavior change interventions in practice: The example of smoking cessation. Journal of Consulting and Clinical Psychology. 2013;81(3):528-44.

96. Michie S, Free C, West R. Characterising the 'Txt2Stop' smoking cessation text messaging intervention in terms of behaviour change techniques. Journal of Smoking Cessation. 2012;7(1):55-60.

97. Lorencatto F, West R, Christopherson C, Michie S. Assessing fidelity of delivery of smoking cessation behavioural support in practice. Implementation Science. 2013;8:40.

98. Gardner B, Whittington C, McAteer J, Eccles MP, Michie S. Using theory to synthesise evidence from behaviour change interventions: the example of audit and feedback. Social Science & Medicine. 2010;70(10):1618-25.

99. Ivers N, Jamtvedt G, Flottorp S, Young JM, Odgaard-Jensen

J, French SD, et al. Audit and feedback: effects on professional practice and healthcare outcomes. Cochrane Database of Systematic Reviews. 2012(6):CD000259.

100. Jamtvedt G, Young JM, Kristoffersen DT, O'Brien MA, Oxman AD. Audit and feedback: effects on professional practice and health care outcomes. Cochrane Database of Systematic Reviews. 2006(2):CD000259.

101. Laba TL, Bleasel J, Brien JA, Cass A, Howard K, Peiris D, et al. Strategies to improve adherence to medications for cardiovascular diseases in socioeconomically disadvantaged populations: a systematic review. International Journal of Cardiology. 2013;167(6):2430-40.

102. Collins LM, Murphy SA, Strecher V. The multiphase optimization strategy (MOST) and the sequential multiple assignment randomized trial (SMART): new methods for more potent eHealth interventions. American Journal of Preventive Medicine. 2007;32(Suppl 5):S112-S8.

103. Webster R, Bailey JV. Development of a theory-based interactive digital intervention to improve condom use in men in sexual health clinics: an application of qualitative methods using the behaviour change wheel. The Lancet. 2013;382:S102.

104. Boutron I, Moher D, Altman DG, Schulz KF, Ravaud P, Group C. Extending the CONSORT statement to randomized trials of nonpharmacologic treatment: explanation and elaboration. Annals of Internal Medicine. 2008;148(4):295-309.

105. Wallace P, Haines A, Harrison R, Barbour J, Thompson S, Jacklin P, et al. Joint teleconsultations (virtual outreach) versus standard outpatient appointments for patients referred by their general practitioner for a specialist opinion: a randomised trial. The Lancet. 2002;359(9322):1961-8.

106. Lee KJ, Thompson SG. The use of random effects models to allow for clustering in individually randomized trials. Clinical Trials. 2005;2(2):163-73.

107. Lorencatto F, West R, Bruguera C, Michie S. A method for assessing fidelity of delivery of telephone-based smoking cessation behavioural support in practice. Journal of Consulting and Clinical Psychology. In press

108. Darnton A, Evans D. Influencing behaviours: a technical guide to the ISM tool. Edinburgh: Scottish Government; 2013.

109. Southerton D, McMeeking A, Evans D. International Review of Behaviour Change Initiatives: Climate Change Behaviours Research Programme. . Edinburgh: Scottish Government Social Research; 2011.

110. Bandura A. Human Agency in Social Cognitive Theory. American Psychologist. 1989;44(9):1175-84.

111. Knott D, Muers S, Aldridge S. Achieving Culture Change: A Policy Framework. London: The Prime Minister's Strategy Unit; 2008.

112. Cochrane Effective Practice and Organisation of Care Group. EPOC resources for review authors. 2010

113. Walter I, Nutley S, Davies H. Developing a taxonomy of interventions used to increase the impact of research. St. Andrews: Research Unit for Research Utilisation; 2003.

114. Abraham C, Kok G, Schaalma H, Luszczynska A. Health Promotion. In: Martin PR, Cheung FM, Knowles MC, Kyrios M, Overmier JB, Prieto JM, editors. The International Association of Applied Psychology Handbook of Applied Psychology. Oxford: Wiley-Blackwell; 2010.

115. Maibach E, Abroms L, Marosits M. Communication and marketing as tools to cultivate the public's health: a proposed "people and places" framework. BMC Public Health. 2007;7:88.

116. Geller S, Berry T, Ludwig T, Evans R, Gilmore M, Clarke S. A conceptual framework for developing and evaluating behavior change interventions for injury control. Health Education Research. 1990;5(2):125-37.

117. Perdue W, Mensah G, Goodman R, Moulton A. A legal framework for preventing cardiovascular diseases. American Journal of Preventive Medicine. 2005;29(5, Suppl 1):139-45.

118. White P. PETeR: a universal model for health interventions. 2010

119. DEFRA. A Framework for Pro-Environmental Behaviours: Report. 2008.

120. Cohen D, Scribner R. An STD/HIV prevention intervention framework. AIDS Patient Care and STDs. 2000;14(1):37-45.

121. Dunton G, Cousineau M, Reynolds K. The intersection of public policy and health behavior theory in the physical activity arena. Journal of Physical Activity & Health. 2010;7(Suppl 1):S91-S8.

122. Goel P, Ross-Degnan D, Berman P, Soumerai S. Retail pharmacies in developing countries: a behavior and intervention framework. Social Science & Medicine. 1996;42(8):1155-61.

123. Vlek C. Essential psychology for environmental policy making. International Journal of Psychology. 2000;35(2):153-67.

124. Population Services International Research Division. PSI Behaviour Change Framework "Bubbles". Washington, D.C.: Population Services International; 2004.

The Behaviour Change Wheel

326

About the authors

Susan Michie

Susan Michie is Professor of Health Psychology, with a background in clinical psychology and organisational change, and Director of the Centre for Behaviour Change (http://www.ucl.ac.uk/behaviour-change) and of the Health Psychology Research Group at University College London, UK. Professor Michie has been a key player in advancing behavioural science and its application to the prevention and management of ill health and the delivery of quality health services, and regularly contributes to national and international policy work. UK examples include co-director of the National Centre for Smoking Cessation and Training; member of NICE's Implementation Strategy Group and of its Behaviour Change Programme Guidance Development Group; Chair of the Behaviour and Communications group of the cross-Government Scientific Pandemic Influenza Advisory Group; member of Public Health England and the Department of Health's Behavioural Insights Expert Advisory Group. For more information, see www.ucl.ac.uk/health-psychology/people/michie/

Lou Atkins

Lou Atkins PhD is a researcher, trainer and consultant in behaviour change intervention design and evaluation in health and environmental sustainability. Dr Atkins is an Associate Teaching Fellow of the Centre for Behaviour Change (University College London, UK) where she leads the teaching programme. She is also a member of the Health Psychology Research Group at University College London. She is involved in a number of projects to: change health professional behaviour, such as reducing variation in adenoma detection rates in colonoscopy; prevent illness, for example reducing cardiovascular disease in people with severe mental illness; and manage illness, such as increasing physical activity in people with musculoskeletal disorders. She is also involved in projects to promote environmental sustainability including increasing recycling in organisations. She is a regular speaker at national and international scientific meetings and in UK Government departments including Department for Work and Pensions and The Treasury. For more information, see http://iris.ucl.ac.uk/iris/browse/profile?upi=LATKI71

Robert West

Robert West is Professor of Health Psychology and Director of Tobacco Studies at the Cancer Research UK Health Behaviour Research Centre, University College London, UK. Professor West is also Editor-in-Chief of the journal Addiction. He has authored more than 500 scientific articles, books and book chapters. He was co-founder of the NHS stop-smoking services. His research includes evaluations of methods of helping smokers to stop and population surveys of smoking and smoking cessation patterns. He is author of 'The SmokeFree Formula' (Orion) which aims to bring the science of stopping to smokers. For more information see www.rjwest.co.uk.

Made in the USA
Columbia, SC
19 March 2024